ECHOES
FROM
LABOR'S
WARS

"He packs more punch and drama
into a few lines than any author we
have read."
— *The Maritime Advocate*

"Dawn Fraser is undoubtedly the
most fearless writer in America."
— *in a Western newspaper*

"This book should be in every house
in Cape Breton and well beyond."
— *Coastal Courier*

"These are songs of rebellion, indig-
nation, hatred of oppression, full of
humour, courage and love of honest
work, songs sung in direct and ro-
bust language."
— *Next Year Country*

Dawn Fraser

ECHOES FROM LABOR'S WARS

THE EXPANDED EDITION

Industrial Cape Breton in the 1920s
Echoes of World War One
Autobiography & Other Writings

WITH AN INTRODUCTION BY
DAVID FRANK & DON MacGILLIVRAY
A CHRONOLOGY & FURTHER READING

Breton Books
Wreck Cove, Cape Breton Island
1992

Echoes From Labor's Wars—
The Expanded Edition

Compilation © Breton Books, 1992

The "Introduction" by David Frank and Don MacGillivray appeared first in the New Hogtown Press edition of *Echoes From Labor's War,* 1977. The cover graphic entitled "Glace Bay" by Lawren Harris is from the *Canadian Forum*, July, 1925, reproduced courtesy of the Lawren Harris Estate. Dawn Fraser's "Autobiography" is from the collection of the Glace Bay Library, Cape Breton Regional Library Board; it was first published in *Cape Breton's Magazine*, Issue 45, June, 1987. "'Oh, You Will Not Drive Over Ben Verick? No, Man, No!'" first appeared in the *Cape Breton Mirror*, July, 1953. "Give Us a Fighting Man" and "I Charge You, British Workers" appeared in the *Maritime Labor Herald* in 1924 and 1926 respectively.

Thanks to Don MacGillivray and David Frank for help and encouragement in compiling the expanded edition.

Production Assistance: Bonnie Thompson
Computer Input: Glenda Watt
Digitalized Photo by Weldon Bona
Printing: City Printers, Sydney

Canadian Cataloguing in Publication Data

Fraser, Dawn, 1888-1968.

Echoes from labor's wars

Subtitle: Industrial Cape Breton in the 1920s; Echoes of World War One; Fraser's autobiography & other stories.
Includes bibliographical references.
ISBN 1-895415-16-0

1. Working class — Nova Scotia — Cape Breton Island — Poetry. 2. World War, 1914-1918 — Canada — Poetry. 3. Fraser, Dawn, 1888-1968 — Biography. 4. Poets, Canadian (English) — 20th century — Biography. I. Title.

PS8511.R274E45 1992   C811'.54   C92-098719-2
PR9199.3.F719E26 1992

Contents

Publisher's Note to the Expanded Edition
by Ronald Caplan

THIS BOOK IS AN EXPANSION of the 1977 version of *Echoes From Labor's War* edited by David Frank and Don MacGillivray for New Hogtown Press—a book centred on the Cape Breton strikes in the 1920s. That slim volume introduced me to Dawn Fraser and sent me out searching for more. Don MacGillivray later brought me a typescript of Fraser's "Autobiography," and I had already located the delicious story Fraser told of his adventures as a travelling salesman in a Cape Breton winter, "Oh, You Will Not Drive Over Ben Verick! No, Man, No!" I wanted to include more poems and stories about Fraser's reluctant experiences in the First World War—often funny, painful narratives. And thus the expansion to *Wars*, to a book twice the size of the text that first won me.

Several years ago, I went to visit a World War One veteran, Mr. Thomas Gillard. He lived in a soldiers' home in Cape Breton. I was collecting stories, and he had been stationed as a forester, cutting wood in France through that war. Somehow the name Dawn Fraser came up. It immediately brightened him. At 90, wearing his legion sportcoat and medals, Mr. Gillard rose to his feet and recited all of "Conscript Brown," a narrative you'll find on page 90—a long poem, and Mr. Gillard knew it all. He recited it standing up, and proud. I knew then that Dawn Fraser belonged to Cape Breton, and to working people. And I knew that Fraser wasn't writing personal, private poems. Mr. Gillard had been indelibly marked, and he in turn touched me. And it is my hope that this little book will mark your life as well.

Fraser's stuff is two-fisted, face-to-face, and strong. No graduate school of English Literature will generate papers on what Dawn Fraser *might* have meant—he meant what he said, and people heard. *Echoes From Labor's Wars* belongs in our homes, and in our schools. It is a powerful, compelling testament to courage, peace, and community.

Introduction: Dawn Fraser & Cape Breton
by David Frank and Don MacGillivray

> His name was Eddie Crimmins
> And he came from Port aux Basques,
> Besides a chance to live and work
> He had nothing much to ask....
> And yet, he starved, he starved, I tell you,
> Back in nineteen twenty-four,
> And before he died he suffered
> As many have before.
> When the mines closed down that winter
> He had nothing left to eat,
> And he starved, he starved, I tell you,
> On your dirty, damned street.

WITH THESE WORDS Dawn Fraser introduced his collection of verse, *Echoes from Labor's War*. Hard and bitter words, to be sure, but the 1920s were hard and bitter years in industrial Cape Breton, and the narrative verse of Dawn Fraser provides us with a remarkably accurate picture of the events and feelings of those years of sharp class conflict.[1]

Few people remember Fraser. Few copies of his published works are available, and two generations of Cape Bretoners are scarcely aware he ever wrote his telling verses about the history of the industrial community. But in the 1920s Fraser was a popular writer in industrial Cape Breton: his particular qualities matched the situation and the people. The oral tradition was still very much a part of the culture and played an important part in preserving working class traditions and values. Fraser belonged to this tradition of storytelling more than to any literary school. He read his verse on the streets, at local union meetings, at parties and at the massive labour and political meetings at the Savoy and Russell Theatres in Glace Bay. His writings appeared in pamphlets, books, magazines and newspapers. For the Glace Bay labour paper, the *Maritime Labor Herald*, he contributed not only stories and verse, but also columns of sports news and advice to the lovelorn. Sometimes his outpourings were simply posted on a bulletin board at the main intersection in Glace Bay. For the workers of industrial Cape Breton, the strong and effective use of language—a sharp tongue or a pointed pun—was one of the weapons at hand. Sharing the principles and prejudices of his community, Fraser was able to articulate common feelings and tell a shared story, and he was an effective and popular presence in the industrial community.

DAWN FRASER WAS BORN ON 1 July 1888 in Oxford, Cumberland County, Nova Scotia, and spent his first years in the Antigonish area. At the turn of the century his family joined the throngs of people attracted to the tremendous industrial expansion taking place in Cape Breton, and moved to Glace Bay in 1901. Some time later the family followed another well-travelled Maritime road to New England, where Fraser began to live and imagine the experiences which form the subject of his earliest writings.[2]

Clues scattered throughout his writings tell us he was at times a male nurse and pharmacist in New England, a labourer in the lumber and construction camps of Maine and New Brunswick, a grave digger, circus barker, copy writer and salesman. A self-confessed drifter, drinker and gambler, he soon began to amuse companions with his natural talent for spinning tales in the style of Robert Service. Fraser's love songs, work songs and drinking songs, and his colourful tales of seamen, labourers, cardplayers and hoboes, show us the excitement and exhilaration of a footloose working class youth on the roam through the Boston States, an experience shared by thousands of Maritimers of Fraser's generation. He later collected these writings as his *Rhymes of the Road*, and there emerges from them a picture of a freewheeling and perceptive individual, scornful of society's pretensions and sympathetic to many of its outcasts and victims.

Then came the First World War. The war ended Fraser's years as a drifter and inserted him into a tragedy for which he cared little. He soon found himself at Camp Aldershot, Nova Scotia, followed by a transfer to a Nova Scotia infantry battalion. "The government became interested in my education," recalled Fraser, "and gave me a free course in the art of bayonet fighting." He was less than impressed with this "barbarous talent," but his verse flourished in the camaraderie of the army camp, and he carried off—he claimed—"all the prizes" at army literary entertainments. Small wonder, for his writings catalogued in clever and amusing verse most of the grievances, small and large, of the enlisted man. Fraser mentioned that he had attained the rank of "Assistant Lance-Corporal," so he was well situated to describe the unpalatable short rations, the worthless canteen checks, the Ross rifles and Kitcheners, the curfews and sick parades that made up the world of the rank-and-file recruit. There was also a host of petty tyrannies, and Fraser's most popular war poem, "The Crime of Johnny Kyle," narrated the history of one particular vendetta between a bullying major and an independent private. In all, Fraser had few kind words for the war or the military. Only the warm winter coats won his approval, prompting a short ode of thanks to Robert Borden.

During his military career, Fraser was part of a small expedition which sailed from the west coast of Canada in December 1918 to participate in the ill-advised Allied effort to quell the Bolshevik Revolution. He spent four months in Siberia, experiencing more of the travails of army life and inventing more adventure yarns and tales, which later made up his *Songs of Siberia*. Here also he learned something of the suffering and determination of a people in the midst of war and revolution. One of the strongest themes in all Fraser's writing was also prompted by the war: the plight of the war veteran, now returned home to more troubles and tragedies. In "The Applicant" he powerfully evokes the fate of one of many gas victims, his health ruined and reduced to seeking public relief. And in "The Reward" we meet another haunting character, Sergeant Gray, hobbling door to door, an embarrassment and a bother to those who reaped benefits from the holocaust. The war changed Fraser. No longer the youthful drifter, he had seen and experienced the dreadful tragedy of war and suffering, and he had learned the costly stupidity of existing politics and authority. He had also forged warm friendships with his fellow Nova Scotians in the army, and he had discovered how popular and powerful his literary talent could be in stirring the emotions and articulating the thoughts of his contemporaries.

He left the army not only with the raw materials for his first book of poetry, but also with a new emotional maturity and a heightened humanity. Upon his release in June 1919, he returned to Glace Bay, where he remembered selling papers on the street as a boy, and working in the mines. He would remain there for the next 40 years. In casting about for a way to earn his living he took up street sales again, becoming an aluminium wares salesman, packing pots and pans door to door and stopping people on the street to read them a rhyme and sell them a book. In the late 1920s he opened his downtown shop, which featured everything from the latest Boston newspapers to dairy products and picture frames, not to mention the latest commentaries of the proprietor. He quickly became an established figure in the town's colourful collection of characters. His virtues and vices would hardly stand out in the industrial community. Men who appreciated a good stiff drink and a well-told story, laced with dry and penetrating wit, could be found in every blind pig, pit and union hall on the island. Fraser soon found new subjects and themes for his verse in the dramatic events of "labor's war."

INDUSTRIAL CAPE BRETON had also changed by the time of the First World War. The years 1917-1926 were a time of increasingly sharp class conflict. They were years of acute industrial crisis as the coal and steel industries, already in decline and badly managed by yet another group of owners, tried in vain to regain the prosperity of the pre-war years. These were also years of cultural crisis for the working class of industrial Cape Breton who, after a generation's experience with large-scale industrial capitalism, had developed a strong and militant trade union movement. The intersection of these two crises produced sharp class conflict, and the industrial crisis tended to accelerate and deepen the cultural crisis.[3]

The most basic and dramatic form of the conflict was the continual attempt of the British Empire Steel Corporation from 1921 on to reduce the wages of the coal miners and to destroy the effectiveness of their new union. These policies were the deliberate measures of a corporation which was itself threatened with imminent collapse because of its flimsy financial structure and its poor market prospects. The coal miners and their families, determined finally to achieve considerable improvements in their standard of living and knowing how much they had already surrendered to the demands of industrial capitalism, refused to accept the wage reductions which corporate logic required. The friction of their incompatible aims produced class conflict.

Even a short glance at the 1920s reveals why Fraser started his collection *Echoes from Labor's War* with "Eddie Crimmins," the unemployed Newfoundlander who died of starvation. Food, or its absence, was an integral element of the conflict. It was a time of undernourished and underfed children, of empty piece cans and barren kitchen cupboards. It was also a time that called forth resistance. As Fraser explained:

> We in Glace Bay are unfortunate in being a one-industry town. Close or suspend operations at the mines and we starve. But before dying we put up a fight, and that is exactly what has happened in this mining area during the dark years referred to.

Putting up a fight: it was a familiar theme in the 1920s in Cape Breton and in Fraser's verse.

Underlying the miners' protracted resistance in the 1920s was an important cultural foundation which had established among the coal miners a pattern of popular beliefs, assumptions and values. By the end of the First World War there existed in the mining communities of industrial Cape Breton a sturdy and independent working class culture, a way of looking at the world characterized by specific ideas about morality, political economy and the community. It was the strength of this culture which provided the energy for the coal miners' long defence of their communities against corporation and government. Fraser's verse was part of this culture, and its basic elements are major themes in his work.

All working class people who have come of age in industrial Cape Breton are early aware that their knowledge of their situation owes far more to their own experience and the teachings of their elders than it does to the system of formal education to which they are subjected. The local school system taught Cape Bretoners how to read and to a certain extent determined what they should read. But the storytellers, the parents, neighbours and friends, were the real custodians of the working class culture of Cape Breton, and it was they who transmitted the values and ideals of that tradition. In one of his earlier efforts, "Out of My House," Fraser introduces us to a wise father, deeply committed to working class principles and bent on teaching them to his son. The father angrily chases a Boy Scout recruiter from the house, showing his firm opposition to militarism in all its forms. The poem announces one of the major themes in Fraser's verse and in the emerging working class culture, namely the end of working class deference and the assertion of an independent working class viewpoint.

Another of Fraser's memorable characters similarly draws on the experience of both war and industrial conflict to announce an independent outlook. The "Widow in the Ward," lying on her deathbed, retells the story of how she lost two sons: one to the foreign war and another to the industrial strife. Her understanding went far beyond forgiveness, and she hurled her condemnation at a world which had brought her this double tragedy. The working class mother and the trade unionist father stand as symbols of the emergence of an autonomous working class viewpoint.

The tradition of deference was a deeprooted cultural one, not easily overcome. Industrialization in Cape Breton in the 19th century had brought about the establishment of a new industrial culture to supplant the preindustrial folkways of a farming and fishing population. The new culture stressed hard work and self-reliance and promised independence and self-fulfillment through faithful and regular toil. Modernizers like the father and son Richard and Richard H. Brown, managers of the General Mining Association, and Robert Drummond, grand secretary of the Provincial Workmen's Association, campaigned vigorously for the establishment of these values against the claims of informal schedules, frequent off-days, disrespect for their betters and undisciplined bouts of rowdiness or drinking. By the 1890s their campaign was to a large degree successful, though when Drummond boasted at the turn of the century of the transformation of the coal miner from the rough, rude and regardless creature of yore into the steady, sober, reliable and faithful employee of the present, one suspects he was still lobbying for the complete achievement of this change.

The rapid expansion of the coal industry and the arrival of large-scale industrial capitalism in Cape Breton in the 1890s generated new tensions. Many coal miners began to think that in order to genuinely achieve those ideals of self-fulfillment and satisfy the claims of individual worth and morality, more effective collective action was necessary. A new cultural conflict emerged, taking the form of disputes between "loyalists" who preached the partnership and harmony of labour and capital, and "rebels" who saw an imbalance, if not direct antagonism, in the relations of labour and capital. The "rebels" campaigned for a more militant and aggressive trade unionism than the leaders of the PWA offered. Where the "loyalists" placed little emphasis on improved wages and living conditions, arguing that for the good of the coal industry the coal miners had to practise restraint in such demands, the "rebels" began to demand priority for these claims, even to the extent of forcing the coal operators to sacrifice some of their profits.[4]

This cultural conflict was the source of the struggle which raged within the PWA from the late 1890s onwards. Ultimately it resulted in the defection of the "rebels" to the United Mine Workers of America, the long and bitter 1909 strike and the reunification of all the coal miners in one union in 1917. By the 1920s there was general agreement among the coal miners that their claims for a better standard of living, what they called a "living wage," should be the first charge on the earnings of the coal industry. The broad acceptance of the "rebel" outlook in the 1920s marked the final abandonment of the old spirit of deference.

The end of the First World War revealed growing class conflict in industrial Cape Breton. This was the golden age of independent labour politics in Nova Scotia and Fraser applauded vigorously as labour candidates won elections to town councils and to the provincial legislature. In 1920 Cape Breton sent four labour MLAs to Halifax and Fraser celebrated the advantages of independent labour politics in "To Forman Waye," a tribute to the most effective member. But politics was simply one manifestation of the changes then occurring in industrial Cape Breton. Fraser portrayed the transformation of labour relations at length in "The Case of Jim McLachlan," his most popular poem of the 1920s. This long poem gives an imaginative reconstruction of the mounting conflict between the coal miners, with their demands for better wages and a larger share of what they produced, and the British Empire Steel Corporation, which insisted on low wages, less work and less wages. Fraser introduces us to some of the leading personalities of the time, including Jim McLachlan, the fiery union secretary-treasurer, and "Roy the Wolf," Besco President Roy M. Wolvin, and he describes many of the actual confrontations and events of the 1920s.

In 1922 Besco attempted to impose a wage reduction of about one-third on its 12,000 coal miners, and the miners' resistance to this demand caused the first major strike of the 1920s. To win a settlement the coal miners used several effective tactics, including the restriction of output by one-third and the enforcement of a 100 per cent strike, in which all workers left the mines. In the wake of this confrontation, the corporation renewed its efforts to weaken the union. The spring of 1923 brought a rampaging provincial police force into industrial Cape Breton, seeking some way to stamp out the apparent red menace which was growing under the influence of the Workers' Party of Canada and the *Maritime Labor Herald*. Fraser narrated the comic opera escapades with relish, printing the adventures in the press as the events unfolded. The summer of 1923 was a dramatic one. The Sydney steelworkers went on strike against Besco at the end of June in an attempt to win union recognition. The provincial police were again sent to Cape Breton and ran riot on Victoria Road on 1 July. They were soon joined by federal troops. The coal miners came out on strike to support the steelworkers and to protest the renewed use of armed force in the industrial area.

For their part in promoting the sympathetic strike the miners' president Dan Livingstone and secretary-treasurer J.B. McLachlan were arrested and jailed. Shortly afterward, the international union, under the leadership of John L. Lewis, deposed the entire union executive and turned the union's charter to the wall. The arrest, trial and conviction of McLachlan for seditious libel provided a host of lessons about the role of the state and the courts in industrial conflict. As Fraser pointed out in "Away False Teachings of My Youth," the basic legal decision in McLachlan's case was that although what he had said might be true, his words were calculated to stir up unrest and therefore he was guilty as charged.

Fraser also articulated the community's hostility towards the repeated invasions of military and police forces. The provincial police, or "Armstrong's Army," were not inaccurately seen as a motley, hastily recruited crew. The unpopularity of the troops was compounded by the peculiarities of the Militia Act, which until 1924 provided that the besieged communities themselves must pay the cost of the military forces. When Glace Bay was billed for the summer invasion of 1923, the town's mayor, Dan Willie Morrison, refused to pay. Fraser expressed the community's feelings on the front page of the *Maritime Labor Herald* with his "Send the Bill to Besco."

One of the remarkable features of class conflict in the coal mining communities was the close identity between class and community interest. Unlike the most evident contemporary parallel, the Winnipeg General Strike, where a violent rift developed between the strikers with their Strike Committee and the middle class with their Committee of

One Thousand, in the mining towns the entire community rallied to the miners' cause. The union and the town shared jointly many of the special functions made necessary by the crisis: the appointment of police, the collection and distribution of relief, the petitioning of provincial and federal governments for the withdrawal of troops and achievement of a fair settlement. This feature was largely a product of the unique social structure of the mining towns: they were very homogeneous working class communities, sharing common experiences, a common employer and often close kinship and ethnic ties. The middle class counter-community was much weaker than in a metropolis like Winnipeg, and indeed much of it was centered in Sydney rather than in the mining towns themselves. By the 1920s the larger mining towns were far from being company towns or small colliery settlements clustered around the pithead. The towns no longer elected company officials or middle class figures as mayors and councillors; instead they elected labour candidates, who engaged in protracted disputes with the coal company over taxes and assessments and services, and supported the union in times of crisis.

The establishment of working class hegemony over the community in Glace Bay was reflected in the writings of Dawn Fraser, who, along with his labour verse, could also pen a pamphlet on behalf of civic progress. In it Fraser attempted to correct the misleading violent image Glace Bay seemed to have acquired in the national press, an image which saw the main streets of the town lined with barrooms from which drunken men stumbled to fight and stain the area with blood. Fraser himself was once asked if it were true that people were commonly killed every pay night at Senator's Corner and the bodies thrown off the cliff at Table Head. Similarly, a staunch middle class figure and civic booster like Stuart McCawley, once an enthusiastic supporter of the British Empire Steel Corporation, could articulate the common hostility to irresponsible outside operators in a pamphlet written at the time of the 1925 strike.[5] The interweaving of community and class in the 1920s provided one more example of the flourishing of a vigorous and independent working class culture.

Another important theme in Dawn Fraser's labour verse is the assertion of an ideology of labour reform. The traditional ideology of labour reform in Canada, as elsewhere in early industrial societies, was "producer ideology," a populist critique of the new industrial order which asserted the ideal of harmony between the truly productive classes of the nation. Producer ideology claimed that labour alone was the source of value, capital being only congealed labour, and this outlook had harsh words for any powerful private interests which would try to extort value from the producers by unfair manipulation of the industrial system. Producer ideology saw no direct exploitation of labour by capital, but rather saw labour and capital as the two legitimate and interdependent partners in industrial life. Such, for instance, was the enduring outlook of the Provincial Workmen's Association when it emerged in Nova Scotia in the late 19th century.[6]

But this ideology could not survive as a single piece the rapid transformation of industrial capitalism in Canada after the 1880s. The two ostensible partners, it was soon discovered, enjoyed grossly unequal bargaining power in their relationship. Reformers began to believe that it was the employers themselves, increasingly large and powerful and usually far removed from the actual process of production, who were responsible for the poverty and hardship of the working class. But although the logic and assumptions of producer ideology were torn apart, some features which were applicable to the new stage of industrial capitalism did survive. The belief in labour as the true source of value persisted, as did the populist assertion of the rights of the community against the powerful monopolies. Fraser's verse expressed this traditional outlook, but also reflected the ways it had been changed and enriched by new developments and perceptions.

Fraser articulated the old aversion to idleness in an aptly named verse, "The Parasites," which is introduced by one of his most quoted comments. The nature of the coal industry itself, where peril and hardship were the price of supplying a basic industrial raw material, encouraged the idea that miners were a vital producing class on which others depended; their claims for fairness and justice frequently took this form. The nature of the dividend system, by which people collected profits from the coal industry not because they did productive work in it but because they owned it through their stocks and bonds, also invited this kind of criticism. It was not difficult for labour spokesmen to prove that, as Fraser put it, "Roy the Wolf and all his clan/ Were a lot of idle, thieving knaves," who were bent on defrauding the public, pillaging the coal industry and robbing the workers. The idea of class partnership found little footing in the swampy land of watered stocks and idle assets. Besco's apparent betrayal of the legitimate and responsible functions of capital encouraged demands that capital be better policed, administered by a public agency or taken over by the workers themselves. The theme that the coal resources belonged by the kindness of God and nature to the people of the area was a popular one among the coal miners of the 1920s, and they deplored the existence of large companies which, by their sheer size and by the weight of their political influence, could assume control of the natural resources and use them for their private profit. Beginning in 1918, when it was adopted as official policy by the miners' union, the coal miners vigorously advocated nationalization of the coal industry.

WHERE DID ALL THIS injustice in industrial society come from? In the first few pages of "The Case of Jim McLachlan," a tale supposedly told to children by an old man in the year 1994, Fraser explained that the earth had become "a rich man's institution" where rules and laws guaranteed profit and privilege for an idle capitalist class. The solution, as Fraser saw it, was class conscious political action to bring in new laws and inaugurate a new social and moral order. Fraser himself stands at the intersection of the old populist producer-oriented critique of industrialism and the emerging socialist critique of industrial capitalism. The traditional ideology accounts for the great tenacity of the "producer," "robbery" and "monopoly" themes in his verse; the socialist influence gives us his view of the problem as one infecting a whole social system, sanctioned by law and requiring political solutions. Fraser's ability to fuse these two outlooks was not unique; indeed it was probably typical of his generation of labour reformers. This fusion of traditional and new approaches gave continuity to a popular intellectual tradition, giving the socialist idea considerable support as a logical evolution of traditional approaches to the problems of industrial society.

The spread of radicalism among the coal miners in the 1920s, which state and corporation so deplored, represented an acceleration and deepening of the longstanding cultural crisis. Many individuals, Fraser included, became "reds," attended "red" events and supported "red" leaders, but it would be misleading to claim that the majority of the miners became committed communists. The "red" phase was too brief and transitory to develop an entirely new radical culture. Nevertheless, the crisis of the 1920s did strengthen and maintain the miners' "rebel" outlook and their populist critique of industrial capitalism. These remained the basic elements of working class culture in industrial Cape Breton for more than a generation. Only since the 1940s, with the general erosion of an independent working class culture throughout the capitalist world, has the culture which Fraser articulated begun to collapse.

The winter of 1924-1925 was the bleakest episode of the 1920s. Low wages and little work meant near-starvation for the miners' families. It is to this hard winter that "Eddie Crimmins" belonged. Fraser himself remembered it as one of the few genuinely hungry periods in his life. Like hundreds of other single young men, Fraser fled the industrial area in search of food and work. Unfortunately we lack a narrative account from Fraser of the hardship and tragedy of the winter and spring of 1925, the long five months' strike which culminated in the battle of Waterford Lake on June 11 with the death of William Davis and the wounding of several more miners, followed by the looting and burning of the company stores and the return of the Canadian Army. In the summer of 1925 the Liberal government was swept out of power and the corporation was finally forced to settle with the coal miners. Fraser returned to the mining community. And while middle class poets like McCawley now tried to drum up enthusiasm for yet another Royal Commission, Fraser had the last word on Besco. During the 1925 strike the expression "standing the gaff" had become a defiant rallying cry among the coal miners. Now, when Besco at last collapsed financially in 1926, the phrase again returned to haunt the corporation in Fraser's "Cape Breton's Curse, Adieu, Adieu."

AFTER THE 1920s Fraser continued to write and publish until the early 1950s, and he remained a well-known personality in Glace Bay. Like the rest of the working population, much of his time was taken up with the problem of earning a living. His writings brought little income, and he made ends meet variously as a salesman, travelling the breadth of the island, or as a picture framer. For a short spell he even had a posting with the federal civil service and for a long time he operated his small shop at Senator's Corner. Here he would post his latest literary and political comments on a bulletin board for the passersby, and the ensuing discussions and debate were a local attraction.

Politics also remained important to Fraser. In 1933, much to the distress of J.S. Woodsworth, he proclaimed himself a candidate for the newly formed CCF and ran in the provincial election. He later was an important force in building local support for the CCF and during the 1940s was campaign manager for Clarie Gillis, the area's first CCF MP. He continued to hawk his literary wares during this time, but his writing dwindled in volume and intensity after *Echoes from Labor's War*. Perhaps this was only one more measure of the way his literary career reflected the shifting mood and spirit of the working class community, for the labour struggles of the 1930s and 1940s never generated the same drama and energy as those of the 1920s.

Eventually Fraser's health failed and he was deemed eligible for the War Veterans' Allowance in 1956. During the last decade of his life he made many long visits to Camp Hill Hospital in Halifax. He died there in June 1968 and his brief obituary made no mention of his writing. But Dawn Fraser's verse, we believe, does deserve to be re-

membered and read, and this small collection will help
serve that purpose.

LITERARY HISTORIANS HAVE PAID too much atten-
tion to the "official" poets in our history and have ignored
the work of the popular local poets like Fraser, who belong
to an entirely different tradition. One of the few critics to
understand this was W.A. Deacon, who in 1927 pointed
out that apart from the "enormous body of intellectualized
poetry" spawned by our "academic-national" poets, there
also existed a vigorous tradition of popular local poetry
which continued in Canadian culture "the great tradition
of the minstrels." This tradition had only a few basic rules:

> that poetry should be simple and grow out of the more
> memorable things in common experience; that any-
> one with natural talent and a yearning to do so may
> make poetry; and that the poetry so made is primarily
> for home consumption, to be directly communicated
> to immediate associates and acquaintances....

"Ignored—indeed, unsuspected—by the literary intel-
lectuals, an army of such poets exists today in Canada, by
their labours emphasizing the fact that the realm of poet-
ry is not a closed preserve for the college-bred; but belongs
equally to the humblest bard who cares to enter it.... In
thousands of villages and hamlets the local poet is as fa-
miliar a figure as the postmaster." Deacon warns us that
"to continue to ignore them is as impossible as it is un-
wise.... If they are hard to classify, that is a problem for
criticism; and the originality of a literary figure was never
yet sufficient cause for ignoring him."[8]
Fraser belonged to none of the orthodox schools of poet-
ry in the Maritimes, neither the academic circles around
the universities in Halifax and Fredericton, nor the con-
genial romantics who banded together as the Song Fisher-
men. He was a loner who rarely thought of himself as a lit-
erary man, and he tended to regard poetry more as a vice
than a vocation. He could on occasion identify himself
rightly with the tradition of Byron, Shelley and Whitman,
but in his heart Fraser probably felt most at home with

the anonymous or little known workingmen's poets who gave Cape Bretoners popular songs like "The Yahie Miners" and "The Honest Workingman" and contributed topical rhyme and commentary to the newspapers, streetcorners and meeting halls of their day.[9] Part of this tradition, Fraser's writing was animated by ideals of morality, by a sense of class and community, and by an aspiration for social and economic reform. His writing reflected the concerns of working class culture in industrial Cape Breton in the 1920s, and at the same time it helped contribute to the coal miners' resistance to the demands of industrial capitalism. And his writings, above all, give us an authentic glimpse of the events, ideas and culture of the 1920s in industrial Cape Breton.

NOTES TO THE INTRODUCTION

1. Fraser published several pamphlets and volumes of verse, among them: *Songs of Siberia* (1919?), *Songs of Siberia and Rhymes of the Road* (1924), *Echoes from Labor's War* (1926), *The Crime of Johnny Kyle and Other Stuff* (192-), *The Case of Jim McLachlan* (192-), *Narrative Verse and Other Comments* (1944?). Much of his verse also appeared in newspapers like the Glace Bay labour paper, the *Maritime Labor Herald*. The present collection is from these sources and represents only a small part of Fraser's writing. Practically all of the verse included here was written in the 1920s, but many of Fraser's introductory comments to the individual poems were written in the 1940s.

2. Fraser was baptized Oswald Vincent Fraser, but the family used Donald and Fraser preferred Dawn. Our sources for biographical data on Fraser included conversations with his widow, Mrs. Mary Fraser, and several residents of Glace Bay who knew Fraser, especially Mr. Maurice MacDonald and Mr. John L. MacKinnon. Also helpful were the Department of Veterans Affairs administration at Camp Hill Hospital, Halifax, and the War Service Records Department, Department of National Defence, Ottawa.

3. For further reading on the history of industrial Cape Breton see Don MacGillivray, "Cape Breton in the 1920s: a Community Besieged" in B.D. Tennyson (ed.), *Essays in Cape Breton History* (Windsor, N.S., 1973), pp. 49-67, "Military Aid to the Civil Power:

the Cape Breton Experience in the 1920s," *Acadiensis*, III:I (Spring, 1974), pp. 45-64, and David Frank, "Class Conflict in the Coal Industry: Cape Breton 1922," in G.S. Kealey and Peter Warrian (eds.) *Essays in Canadian Working Class History* (Toronto, 1976), pp. 161-184, 226-231.

4. "Loyalist" and "rebel" attitudes are discussed in an article about the history of the American working class: Alan Dawley and Paul Faler, "Working Class Culture and Politics in the Industrial Revolution, 1820-1890," *Journal of Social History*, IX:4 (June, 1976), pp. 466-480.

5. Dawn Fraser, *If We Saw Ourselves as Others See Us: The Truth About Glace Bay and Other Mining Communities* (Glace Bay, 192-), Stuart McCawley, *Standing the Gaff: The Soreness of the Soul of Cape Breton* (Glace Bay, 1925).

6. For an example of nineteenth century labour reform ideology see T. Phillips Thompson, *The Politics of Labor* (1887, Toronto, 1975). Labour ideology is discussed briefly in L.R. MacDonald, "Merchants against Industry: An Idea and Its Origins," *Canadian Historical Review*, LVI:3, (September, 1975), especially pp. 278-280.

7. J.S. Woodsworth to A.B. MacDonald, 14 March 1935, J.S. Woodsworth Papers, Vol. 3, Public Archives of Canada.

8. W.A. Deacon, *The Four Jameses* (1927, Toronto, 1974), p. 190, p. 196. For later discussions of the popular tradition in Canadian literature see V.G. Hopwood, "Have We a National Literature?" *New Frontiers*, V:1 (Spring, 1956), pp. 12-17 and David Arnason, "Comment," *Journal of Canadian Fiction*, II:2, (Spring, 1973), pp. 1-2.

9. The tradition of the preindustrial bard in Nova Scotia is discussed by C.W. Dunn in *Highland Settler* (Toronto, 1953; reprinted with additional readings by Breton Books, 1991); a similar dimension in Upper Canada is represented by Alexander McLachlan, who is discussed by Ken Hughes in "Poet Laureate of Labour," *Canadian Dimension*, XI:4 (March, 1976), pp. 33-40 and "The Completeness of McLachlan's 'The Emigrant,'" *English Studies in Canada*, 1:2 (Summer, 1975), pp. 172-187. Fraser's contemporaries included Dannie Boutilier of Springhill and George Straatman of Springhill, Westville and Florence. Today the tradition is carried on by ballad singers and writers like Ronnie MacEachern of Sydney.

PUBLISHER'S NOTE: In September, 1987, Fraser's verse was central to "Tough Times," a song and poetry performance at the Savoy Theatre in support of the Glace Bay Food Bank. "Tough Times" was organized and directed by Joella Foulds; actor Gary Walsh portrayed Dawn Fraser.

For recent work on the theme of traditional oral culture in Cape Breton see David Frank, "The Industrial Folk Song in Cape Breton," *Canadian Folklore canadien*, VIII, Nos. 1-2 (1986), 21-42, and his chapter "Tradition and Culture in the Cape Breton Mining Community in the Early Twentieth Century," in K. Donovan, ed. *Cape Breton at 200* (Sydney, 1985), 203-218; and Don MacGillivray's "The Industrial Verse of 'Slim McInnis,'" *Labour / LeTravail*, 28 (Autumn, 1991), 271-83, and his "Glace Bay: Images and Impressions," in B. H. D. Buchloh, R. Wilkie, eds., *Mining Photographs and Other Pictures* (Halifax, 1983), 171-191.

See also John O'Donnell's *And Now the Fields are Green: A Collection of Coal Mining Songs in Canada*, University College of Cape Breton Press, 1992; and the article dealing in part with songwriter/miner Phil Penny, "'George Alfred Beckett': Story and Song," in *Cape Breton's Magazine*, June (1986), 53-62.

Further readings in Cape Breton's Industrial Wars and Cape Bretoners in World War One include: David Frank, "From Company Town to Labour Town," in *Histoire Social / Social History*, Vol. XLV, No 27, May, 1981; reprinted in *Cape Breton's Magazine*, Issue 37, August, 1984; and "The Trial of J.B. McLachlan," *Communication historiques / Historical Papers* (1983).

Sara M. Gold, "A Social Worker Visits Cape Breton," *Social Welfare;* reprinted in *Cape Breton's Magazine*, Issue 38, January, 1985.

Paul MacEwan, *Miners and Steelworkers: Labour in Cape Breton*, Samuel Stevens Hakkert & Company, Toronto, 1976.

"The 1923 Steelworkers' Strike and the Miners' Sympathy Strike," *Cape Breton's Magazine*, Issue 25, June, 1979.

"The 'Pluck Me': Life and Death of the Company Store," *Cape Breton's Magazine*, Issue 3, March, 1973.

"Cape Bretoners in World War One," *Cape Breton's Magazine*, Issues 33 and 34, June and August, 1983.

Part 1

Echoes from Labor's War—
Industrial Cape Breton
in the 1920s

A Short Chronology

1879 Formation of the Provincial Workmen's Association, the first coal miners' union in Nova Scotia

1893 Establishment of the Dominion Coal Company, marking the arrival of large-scale industrial capitalism in the Nova Scotia coalfields

1909 The Nova Scotia coal miners strike for recognition of the United Mine Workers of America

1919 Establishment of District 26, UMWA, in Nova Scotia and New Brunswick

1920 Formation of the British Empire Steel Corporation (Besco)

1922 The coal miners resist a one-third wage reduction imposed by Besco

1923 The coal miners strike in sympathy with the steelworkers of Sydney, who are fighting for recognition of their union

1924 Coal miners resist a 20 percent wage reduction

1925 Coal miners again resist a 20 percent reduction

1926 Besco begins to collapse. New management takes over in 1928 and the Dominion Steel and Coal Corporation takes control in 1930

He Starved, He Starved, I Tell You

His name was Eddie Crimmins
And he came from Port aux Basques,
Besides a chance to live and work
He had nothing much to ask;
No, not a dream he ever had
That he might work and save—
Was quite content to live and die
And be a working slave.
And yet, he starved, he starved, I tell you,
Back in nineteen twenty-four,
And before he died he suffered
As many have before.
When the mines closed down that winter
He had nothing left to eat,
And he starved, he starved, I tell you,
On your dirty, damned street.

The papers told of how the prince
Had caught a little cold,
And how the princess' youngest kid
Was nearly four years old;
Such news is featured foremost
In every yellow sheet,
But they don't tell when workers die
Standing on their feet;
Standing on their feet because
Nowhere to lay their head.
No, such news ain't featured much—
I bet you never read
How for days young Crimmins
Wandered round the street,
And how a half-froze apple
Was the last he had to eat.

Too poor to buy, too proud to beg,
He sunk down like a log,

You never threw the lad the crust
You'd throw a lonely dog.
Oh Capital! oh Capital!
You've an awful debt to pay—
Oh Capital, I hope it's true
There is a judgment day;
And when the great judge calls you up,
May I be there to see,
And if he wants a witness
I hope he calls on me.
If I have wings, I'll gladly fly,
If not, I'll use my feet,
And then I'll tell how Crimmins died
Upon your damned street.

I Write Not What I Wish to Write But Rather What I Must

I write, not what I wish to write,
But rather what I must;
My many imperfections
You will pardon, friends, I trust.
I cannot write to order
By plan or measure given,
My dreams come rushing o'er me
As by a tempest driven.
You do not blame the tempest
Because perchance it screams—
And will you blame the dreamer
Because the dreamer dreams?
Vain might I seek for "lofty thoughts,"
Vain seek the "noble soul"—
How can I offer what I lack?
How can I thoughts control?
Thoughts fantastic in their course
That, as they travel, gather force.

I am like a boy who shakes a tree
With many an apple fair to see—
The ripe fruit showers round his head,
He views his act with awe and dread;
And yet the deed no lesson taught,
The consequence is soon forgot;
Despite all punishment or pain,
He will shake that tree some day again.
So, gentle friends, it is with me—
I am about to shake the tree.
The fruit of this strange tree is verse,
And some is bad and some is worse.
It tumbles down—disordered rhyme—
(To call them poems might be a crime);
And yet I ask, may it not be
That somewhere hidden in that tree

Are some few truths, wholesome and sound?
Oh! could I bring them to the ground,
Though root and trunk and branches break,
I'd give that tree a mighty shake.

And so I sit and write and write,
Through all the day and half the night;
My fancy carries me away—
I see strange lands as plain as day;
Put pen or pencil in my reach,
I visit Europe or Palm Beach.
I see it all in clear detail
And could describe it without fail—
Describe it as it seems to be
In my imagination free.
Ah! little book, 'twas in my mind
To have you gentle, true and kind;
To fill your soul with wit and fun,
And yet speak well of everyone.
To call the world a paradise,
('Tis so our schools instruct the youth)
But, oh! alas! that's not the truth;
And if I catch you lying ever,
I'll tear your heart from out of your cover.

Among the masses I am one
Who never had a natural son;
You, product of my fancy wild,
With all your faults, you are my child.
I take a father's pride in you,
I'd have you honest, lad, and true,
Courageous, honest, free and bold—
Truth is more precious, son, than gold.
We scorn the base pen-parasite
Who for a wage betrays the right;
Such souls are peddled, sold and bought
To duplicate their masters' thought.

A man in chains may yet be brave,
The meanest is the mental slave;
Shame upon the ink-stained slob
Who only writes to please the mob.
Here is a truth, lad, known to few—
Ideas are cleanest when they are new;
It's best to parade them at their birth,
They grow stained on the vulgar earth;
But if their source, the mind, is clean,
They are like to flourish ever green;
Parade them then in justice cause
And be suspicious of applause.
Perfect this lesson in your youth—
You win few laurels speaking truth;
Such products often sting and hurt—
You will find more sale for lies and dirt.

We will run this race, lad, unattached,
The others are unfairly matched,
So weighted down in soul and mind—
G'dap! we'll leave them far behind.
The man is beaten to his knees
Who hesitates and strives to please,
Who blends a mess of truth and lies
That he may win the Nobel Prize;
Who sacrifices honest thought
To catch the nod from some Big Shot.
Oh! pass such trifles up, my boy,
That you may know the keener joy
Of writing freely, day by day,
And let the chips fall where they may.
When thoughts are launched unselfishly
They are more likely true to be,
And writing is a worthy game
When one scorns gold, applause and fame;
But he who sets these as his goal
May win them all, but lose his soul.

Out of My House.
No Child of Mine Will Be a Boy Scout

My Father was a carpenter,
Who worked hard every day.
His back was bowed, his hands were hard,
His locks were thin and grey.
That was many years ago.
The Locals then were small.
And every man who met the Boss
Would touch his hat and crawl.
But Father had a rebel's heart.
And often he told me
Of how he hoped I'd see the day,
When workers would be free.

I went to school each morning.
But most that they taught me
Was how old England licked the world,
And was mistress of the sea.
Of Wolfe and Blake and Nelson,
Half the day they would brag.
And tell how glorious it was
To die beneath some flag.
They would tell us of the Dargia Heights
And of Majuba Hill.
They taught it was a noble act
To kill and kill and kill.

One day we had a visitor
Of military mien.
He had the slickest uniform
We kids had ever seen.
He gave a little lecture
And it was all about
How would we like to go to camp?
And be a Boy Scout?
We would march each day, away, away.

It would be jolly fun.
We would get a pretty uniform
And maybe have a gun.

I ran right home to father
And hopped upon his knee.
I was going to be a scout.
Wasn't he proud of me?
The man would call, the teacher said,
And fix it up with Dad.
She said she knew each Parent
Would be most proud and glad.
But Daddy didn't hear the news
With any show of pride.
He kind of hugged me tighter
And then he kind of sighed.

One evening I was playing home
With what little friends I had.
The military fellow called
And asked to see my Dad.
But when my Father spied him,
This well dressed Master Scout,
My Father grabbed the poker
And I heard my Father shout.
Out of my house. No child of mine
Will be a Boy Scout.
Out of my house you useless tool
I know what you're about.
The soldier of tomorrow
Is the Boy Scout of today.
Our very blood and bones you'd use
Against us in the fray.
You rob the worker of his child
And dress him like a clown.
You put a gun into his hands,
To shoot his father down.

Give you a child of mine to train?
You take me for a fool.
You keep your hands off me and mine
You capitalist tool.

That military man so grand
Was timid as a mouse
Last thing I remember,
Father chased him from the house.
And then he took me in his arms
And kissed me once or twice.
I never saw him cross before,
He was always sad but nice.
Before I went to bed each night,
He would tell me stories fine.
And the one he told that evening
Was about the HOMESTEAD MINE.
Somewhere far away, he said,
There was a little town
Where he had seen the soldiers come
And shoot the workers down.

Publisher's Note: Dawn Fraser's image refers to the
1892 strike at the Carnegie Steel Works in Homestead,
Pennsylvania.

The Widow in the Ward

No, I can't forgive them, parson,
Here on my dying bed,
Them as calls me "the crazy widow"
And say I am out of my head.
Let it pass, what they calls me—
It's not the worst they have done;
I'll always hold it ag'in them
For killing my second son.
With Harry, he was different,
I know the boy was wild;
Maybe I was most to blame,
When he was a little child.
Maybe I was over-kind
And let him run too free;
But they don't understand a mother—
He was always kind to me.
'Twas full of life the lad was,
Roaming the night and day,
Brave and happy and careless,
Easily led astray.
'Twas bad companions spoiled him
With cards and dice and drinks;
It's a wonder when one gets started,
How quickly a mortal sinks.

Then the labor trouble started,
The men were out on strike,
Riots and pickets and scabbers—
You never saw the like.
And my Harry was a leader,
Working the night and day,
With little hope of winning,
Without a penny of pay.
Desperate and starving the boy was,
Times were terrible bad—
And though he shot a policeman,
There was no real harm in the lad.
Then the dark days of trouble

When he was taken to jail;
No one to offer him counsel,
No one to offer him bail,
Except the lawyer the Crown appointed
To take and plead his case—
He was the most ag'in him—
It was a clean disgrace.
And black Judge James presiding,
Him with the evil eye,
'Twas only what all expected—
The boy was sentenced to die.

And one dark morning it happened—
God! but it seemed hard—
They took my boy and hanged him
Out in the court house yard.
And, parson, I never murmured—
I was younger and stronger then—
And the law must be abided
By the best and worst of men.
And I still had little Thomas,
He was my pride and joy;
I prayed to God to help me
To bring up my little boy.
He seemed different from Harry,
Pretty and gentle and mild,
His rougher companions called him
The "widow's angel child."
And so he grew to manhood,
Working hard each day,
Coming home each week-end
And bringing me home his pay;
Trying to help his mother,
But they wouldn't give him a chance;
They killed him the same as Harry,
As they told me, "Somewhere in France."
What was the use of trying,
And fretting about my son?
They fattened him up and killed him
Just like the other one.

It was a common murder
I'll say it my dying day—
Very same policeman came for him
That took poor Harry away.
Conscripting the lad to make him fight,
Such action I never saw;
After I always told him
To fight was ag'in the law.
What was the use of trying?
I wouldn't try anymore—
Making him do the very thing
They hanged his brother for.

Away to some camp they took him,
Took him ag'in his will,
Training and feeding him all the time,
Getting him ready to kill.
He had no trial like Harry,
No, not as good a chance—
Just carried him off and killed him
Over somewhere in France.
They confessed it in the telegram
And the letter they sent along—
Said they were sorry for it;
Don't that show they were wrong?
And they wanted to give me money
To make up the wrong they done—
Forty dollars a month they said
Was the price of my son.
But I couldn't take money for him
Now that the deed is done;
And I'll never forgive them, parson,
For killing my second son.

The Applicant

It's very kind of you, Mum, to call to see my Dan.
Since he came back he seems to be a very wreck of
    man;
I think it must be German gas, still inside his head,
He talks of places back in France and lads that now
    are dead.
Oh, thank you for the flowers—I'll put them with the
    rest—
Would you believe, he seems to like these maple
    leaves the best;
And yet when he's beside them, it's awful how he
    grieves,
And often I have heard him talking to the leaves.
Sometimes he will be laughing, then again he'll sob,
And talking to the leaves about the way he done his
    job.
You see, he went away to France, he and his brother
    Joe;
I didn't try to stop them, they wanted so to go.
That's more than four years gone now, when the war
    begun,
It seemed every mother's duty to give away her son.
But when I think about it, it makes me very sad—
Dan looked so big and grand that day, and now he
    looks so bad.
And they fought in different countries—France,
    Belgium and in Somme,
In Vimy, Flanders, Passchendaele—but now poor
    Joe is gone;
No doubt you heard about it, the papers all were
    filled,
Was in this place they call the Somme that my boy
    Joe was killed.
But Dan is only bad at times when the gas is in his
    head,

When he came in the other day I remember what he
    said;
It's only when he loses heart that the poor lad really
    grieves,
And then he will start all over, talking to the leaves.
About the last job he had, and how he done his best;
He has his recommend with him, the button on his
    breast.
Talks about the trenches, the cold and wounds and
    pain,
How he starved and waited; now must he starve
    again?
He says how in the morning he must see another
    man—
It's very kind of you, Mum, to call to see my Dan.

The Reward

The following rhyme was written with prophetic vision early in 1917. We do not claim that the condition is general, but we do say that it is not uncommon. It is an open question among returned men today whether to wear the button is an advantage or otherwise. Our own attitude is undecided, but we certainly have heard returned men say that displaying the button handicaps them socially and in a business way. An old lady told me that she would not have returned men around her house, as anybody who was full of cooties for four years was likely to have an odd one still about his person. Perhaps there is some excuse for this idea, but is it not a sad condition to find that returned men are hiding their buttons as if they were ashamed of them?

'Twas a western town—but no matter—'twas not the
    fault of the town—
Time was—well, no matter—'twas after the sun went
    down;
'Twas after the war was over, and in a crowded
    saloon,
Crowds that were feasting and drinking, the orches-
    tra playing a tune.
But there was one in the party who did not seem to
    belong,
His gaze was shifty and timid, like one who had got
    in wrong;
One wasted arm hung over a crutch, one eye had a
    look of despair;
The other arm off at the elbow—the other eye wasn't
    there.
He staggered up to the counter, with features faded
    and gaunt,
The boss looked up with disfavor and growled,
    "What d'ya want?"
"If you'd spare a coin for some food, sir, I am weary
    of travelling too,

I am something of a cripple, you see, and it's hard to
get work to do;
Before the war it was different—before I was hit by
the bomb—
I have been some time in France, sir, and lost my
arm at the Somme."

"We don't lend money," the boss replied, "more like
you want it for rum—
That story is old as hell—we get it from every bum.
Last night 'twas a drunken brakeman, careless with
his fool neck,
Couldn't let the booze alone and got mixed up in a
wreck.
I don't want to see your button—beat it and stow
your gaff!"
I saw him wave the man away, I heard the gay
crowd laugh;
Thus encouraged, the boss went on, with a kind of
injured glance:
"As if I could afford to pay the board of every cripple
from France."
And his prosperous patrons agreed with him—said
something should be done—
That since the war these bums were a bore, a
menace to everyone.
Then I saw the cripple clutch his crutch and tap his
way to the door,
And it struck me then, but I couldn't say when, I'd
seen the man before.
He seemed to be sort of shy of me, afraid he wouldn't
be heard,
But I'd bet my pay 'twas Sergt. Gray, who crossed
with the 93rd.

I had last seen Gray one summer day, one early morn
in June,

And remembered then how these very men had
　　cheered for his platoon.
One of the first when the war-cloud burst, when the
　　call to arms was heard,
He forgot his all at the nation's call, and joined the
　　93rd.
There were others too, and not a few—men who
　　risked their all,
Left home and friends, threw careers to the winds, to
　　answer the country's call.
These volunteers gained the country's cheers, their
　　names were on every tongue,
When they sailed away that summer's day, the
　　heroes of old and young;
And I wondered why, if to do or die he bravely
　　marched away,
His standard fell, when shot to hell, he stood in the
　　town today.
And the very men who were shy of a gun, and
　　ducked at the great showdown,
And riches sought, while others fought for their
　　country, home and town,
Were the men today of the party gay, who laughed
　　and failed to heed
When the hero bright of another night wanted a stake
　　or a feed.

It's not every cheer that is all sincere, but a means to
　　a selfish end,
And the vulgar crowd with acclaims aloud is not
　　always your friend.
If you do the work that others shirk, if you play the
　　willing goat,
They tolerate and declare you great, while the medals
　　shine on your coat.
As long as you live and have something to give—your
　　comfort, your wealth or your time,

You'll find these friends with selfish ends to trim
      you down to a dime;
But lose your wealth, or lose your health, or show
      any signs of wear,
Get knocked about, or down and out, and the cheers
      are no longer there.
In this world of sin you've got to win, and you can't
      get by on a past;
While you're fit for strife, for war to the knife, so
      long will your glory last.

The Case of Jim McLachlan
(A story told the children by an old man in the year 1994)

Listen, my children, and you shall know
Of a crime that happened long ago,
In the dark and dismal days of old
When the world and all was ruled by Gold,
When the earth was a rich man's institution—
That was before the Revolution—
When the gold was dug by the toiling masses
But stolen from them by the master classes.
Yes, men went way down under the ground
And hunted and toiled till the gold was found;
And it sometimes happened to these men
That the earth fell in and buried them,
But still others toiled on, both young and old,
Working, working to get the gold.

But there was another class, I recall,
Who never did any work at all—
Sat in rich offices 'bove the ground,
Yet they got all the gold was found.
How did they get it? You want to know—
Were they stronger than those who worked below?
Did they beat in combat the other men?
No, dear, the gold was handed them.
Yes, the workers who dug in every land
Crawled up and laid the gold in their hand,
And the reason they did it was because
There was a thing they called "the laws";
And the law was, in these days of old,
That the lazy men owned all the gold
And all the minerals in the ground
Belonged to them, wherever found;
And these rules, of course, were made because
'Twas the lazy men who made the laws,
And they were given this easy job
By the very men they used to rob.
Yes, children, it's hard for you to see
How such conditions could ever be,

But I have seen Election Day
When working men would shout "Hurray!"
Would vote, would argue—yes, and fight
For the Hon. Carroll and Hon. Kyte.
They would choose these men to make the laws
That acted against the workers' cause,
And once when there was a strike in town,
These men sent soldiers to ride them down.

Thus the lazy bosses piled up their gains
'Til the workers began to use their brains;
Very slowly it dawned on them
That the lazy ones were cheating them
And robbing them of the treasures they found
By working so hard beneath the ground.
And after a time the working mass
Spoke of these thieves as the "Capitalist Class"—
Certain workers saw through the plan,
And Jim McLachlan was such a man;
He told the men they were being fooled
By the other Capitalist Class that ruled;
He organized workers and trained them well,
And he told the bosses to go to hell.
Ah! he was an honest, fearless man,
And he fought the bosses when trouble began.

Oh, yes, it's true—I should have told
That the workers were given a little gold;
Yes, every week, on a certain day,
They were given something was called their "pay."
'Twas a very small part of the gold they found
By working so hard beneath the ground.
I have said that the world was ruled by gold,
And it was for it that goods were sold—
Food and clothing and everything
Was bought for gold, and gold was king;
So the workers were given a little. Why?
If they didn't have food of course they'd die;
And if the working class was dead,
How would the capitalist class be fed?

That was the reason they gave them pay,
To keep them alive from day to day,
With strength enough to dig the ground
So the master class could bum around.

Well, as long as they had enough to eat,
The workers toiled on with weary feet,
Like faithful horses or patient saints,
Without demands or without complaints:
Day by day they would toil and strive,
Satisfied just to keep alive.
And as I have said, on election night
They would cry, "Hurrah for Carroll and Kyte!"
And send these men to Ottawa
To tinker 'round about the law,
And year after year, each law they'd pass
Tightened the chains on the working class.

So the capitalist class owned all the gold,
And they also owned the goods that were sold,
Controlling the workers in every way,
And they grew greedier day by day;
'Til they thought of a little scheme was good—
They raised the prices of all the food,
So that the workers with pay they got
Couldn't pay for the goods they bought;
Couldn't pay for the bread and meat
That they and their families needed to eat;
Though they worked long hours and longer yet,
There were things they needed and couldn't get;
But the capitalist class had many things—
Motor cars and diamond rings—
Yet all these riches, wherever found,
Were dug by the workers from the ground,
Were stolen from them by this thieving band—
Such was the law in all the land.

Now, of all the bosses that e'er were cursed,
Roy the Wolf was called the worst,
He was the leading parasite

That fed on the workers day and night;
Greedy, growling wolf for more,
He stole the bread from the workers' door,
Grew fat on starving children's cries
And filled the papers with foolish lies—
That his company couldn't afford to pay—
Yet he got three hundred dollars a day
For doing nothing but looking wise,
Starving kids and telling lies;
Thus he promoted the capitalist game
'Til babies were taught to curse his name,
And Roy the Wolf and his thieving band
Spread distress throughout the land.

But Jim McLachlan and other men
Saw that something must be done,
And they started one of the many fights
For labor's cause and labor's rights,
And they called on Roy the Wolf to give
More of the gold that they might live,
More of the gold they had to pay
To meet the prices from day to day;
And they got a little more gold for the men,
But then the prices went up again,
'Til the workers began to blame the laws
That acted always against their cause;
And they blamed the men at Ottawa
Who were sent up there to fix the law.
They organized and made a fight
Against the members, Carroll and Kyte,
And the very men they used to cheer
Were greeted now with a hiss and a jeer.

And they thought that maybe to change the law
They would send McLachlan to Ottawa;
And thus when another election came,
The working men got into the game.
McLachlan was fighting and running strong,
And but for a cowardly, cruel wrong,
When somebody told a lot of lies

To fool the workers and blind their eyes.
There used to be men, and there are still,
Who never had brains and who never will;
So believing these lies, the working men
Voted for Carroll and Kyte again—
Electing the men who made the laws
That acted always against their cause;
And McLachlan lost when they counted the vote,
And capital still was at labor's throat.

But brave McLachlan was not dismayed,
He knew the game and how 'twas played,
Never yellow and never sore,
When they had him down he fought the more;
Struggling always for labor's cause,
Fighting against the rich man's laws,
Exposing the capitalist parasite
That fed on the workers day and night;
And he told the workers, man to man,
That Roy the Wolf and all his clan
Were a lot of idle, thieving knaves
Who held the workers the same as slaves,
That even Negro slaves of old,
Who were peddled 'round and bought and sold,
Who were never given any pay,
Were better off than the men today.
The cruelest driver of workers knows
That slaves must have shelter, food and clothes—
Yes, and they used to get them. Why?
If they didn't eat, the slaves would die;
And as Negro slaves belonged to the boss,
Of course their death was a serious loss.

It's the same with a man who owns a horse—
He gives him food to eat, of course,
If he wants him to breed and haul and drive,
He has to keep the horse alive.
But the capitalists have a cheaper plan
In their scheme of things with the working man,
He does not really belong to the boss,

So if he starves he is no real loss,
Or if he's killed while digging the ground
Another slave is easily found;
To recruit new workers from every nation
They encourage a thing called "IMMIGRATION."

All this McLachlan told the men,
And the battle was renewed again;
Bravely still the workers fought,
Fighting for every crust they got;
Prices went up from day to day,
Still the bosses wanted to cut the pay.
A strike was pulled by working men,
And brave McLachlan fought for them;
He pulled the cleverest trick of the age,
The bosses called it "SABOTAGE."
Biggest and last of labor's trumps,
It took the workers off the pumps,
It drew the timber-men from the mine,
And all who worked in every line.
Now, where these tactics are employed,
Of course the mine will be destroyed,
The master class will lose their hold,
The capitalists will lose their gold.

Then Roy the Wolf began to weep,
His tears fell fast, his groans were deep—
"I don't care what you do to me,
But, oh! protect my property!"
All this was music sweet to Jim,
McLachlan only laughed at him;
Says he, "It's no affair of mine,
Go ahead and save your mine;
You never saved a worker's child,
In your damn mine good men have died,
Good men were crippled—yes, for life,
So that your children and your wife
Might live in comfort, ease and health,
Enjoy the luxuries of wealth.
Your children pass their time in schools

Learning new tricks to trap the fools;
Some day they will help to make the laws,
New rules to cripple labor's cause;
Labor must nurse this parasite,
Her future enemy in the fight.

"Listen, Wolf, when I was nine,
I trapped a door down in a mine,
I never knew a childish joy,
A slave while still a little boy.
They took me and my humble friends
And picked our bones for dividends.
Why should I save your property?
I tell you it don't interest me.

"Go, wake your boy, your pride and hope,
And lead him to yon lonely slope,
Some morning chill, ere dawn appears,
And laugh away his childish fears;
Tell him to guard yon trap-door well,
Then chase him down, half way to hell,
Leave him on some dark headway,
To cry his eyes out half the day,
Let him hear the pillars groan
As he crouches there alone,
'Til some passing miner's light
Half relieves his childish fright.
Feeble light soon disappears,
With the dark return his fears;
Leave him there for seven hours,
Treat your child the same as ours;
Leave him weary, cold, half-fed—
Do you wonder we see red?
If you want to save your mine,
Here is a paper you must sign;
Sign this contract for to give
Wages that will let us live,
Food and clothing, shelter too,
And we will work our best for you.
You may keep your ill-got gains—

Labor now is used to chains.
While your family sports around,
We will toil beneath the ground;
But, failing this, now hear me well,
You and your mine can go to hell!"

But, children, perhaps I weary you—
A little more and I'll be through.
I know it's hard to understand
How evil men owned all the land.
How did they get it all? you say—
The government gave it away;
You see, the men who make the laws,
Were friendly to the capitalist cause;
They were all college chums, you see,
And owned stock in the company.
They raised an awful howl then
About McLachlan and his men—
Called them traitors and everything,
Said they plotted against the King;
And they even had the unlimited gall
To say the mines were not theirs at all—
It served their purpose then, you see,
To call them the people's property;
Yet while men toiled in peaceful times,
Roy the Wolf owned all the mines.
Oh, they were a precious pack of knaves
Who held the workers the same as slaves.

Yes, Roy the Wolf had many friends
To do his bidding and serve his ends—
Judges, lawyers and politicians
Favored him always with decisions—
You see they belonged to the lazy breed
Who never work but who always feed—
And many of them had stock, you see,
With Roy the Wolf and company.
So they gathered up a lot of bums,
Crooks and drifters from the slums,
Dressed them pretty and soldier-like,

And sent then down to break the strike;
Called them police—oh, it was a shame—
A stain on any government's name.
For one Sunday night in a certain town
This mob beat people and rode them down—
Helpless people who all unarmed
Thought they might walk the street unharmed.
Oh, it was a shame that a peaceful land
Should be given over to such a band.

What occurred on the city street that night
Spelled defeat for Carroll and Kyte,
Though they made excuses and often ran,
They got no more votes from the working man.
Now, McLachlan wanted everyone
To know what these mongrel police had done,
So he sent a letter around the land
Warning the workers on every hand
To beware of Armstrong's evil band.
This Armstrong was the governor stern,
And he had a henchman named O'Hearn.
And they had a crony who was a judge,
And they held in common a kind of grudge
Against McLachlan, and they said
He was an agitating Red;
All the trouble was caused by him,
So they framed a plot to get poor Jim.

O'Hearn sought many a mouldy book,
Scanning the law with saintly look—
Read through all the ancient pages,
Records of the darker ages;
Records that were quite revealing
(They used to hang a man for stealing)
And farther back than that he saw
To tell the truth was 'gainst the law,
And so a warrant was sworn and given
For Jim McLachlan, dead or living;
He was arrested and lodged in jail,
The crony judge refused him bail.

Now, would you think that could be done
Anywhere beneath the sun?
It's truth I tell, it happened so,
And not so very long ago.

The papers all had held a piece,
How men were beaten by the police;
Every father, mother, brother,
Had told the story to each other.
Yes, everywhere about the street,
Any man that you would meet,
Would tell the truth—could not be hid—
An awful thing those policemen did;
Story was told, re-told, attested,
But McLachlan only was arrested;
Yes, he and just one other man
Whom the workers called "Red Dan."
But soon O'Hearn let Dan go,
Which only served to better show
How all the tyrants' hate was sped
At noble Jim McLachlan's head.

Much of the trial I need not tell—
'Twill be reviewed some day in hell;
McLachlan sat with lofty scorn
And heard his enemy, O'Hearn
Repeat the joke of all the time—
To tell the truth was foul crime.
Truth divine to justice cause
Must be enslaved to capitalist laws.
Yes, "It's a fact," O'Hearn said,
Or from some foolish paper read,
How in some cases that he saw,
To tell the truth was 'gainst the law.
I've heard a witness for Jim,
When he was being sworn in,
Asked the judge what he should do,
For if he told him what was true,
If he told him what he saw,
Perhaps it would be against the law.

Some truths it seemed that he might tell,
But others must be hidden well.
The information that he sought
Was what to tell and what to not.

No, of the trial I will not tell—
It has a most unpleasant smell;
Too often evil will prevail—
They sent McLachlan back to jail.
They could as easily shot or strung him—
The wonder is they never hung him.
Children, I'm old, but in my time,
I've never heard of such a crime.

The day that Jim McLachlan fell
The workers should have tolled a bell,
Well might they weep, ah, bitter tears,
Their cause went back a hundred years.
Ah! starving, patient, helpless men,
You'll never find his like again.
Bend, Labor, bend; pick up your cross;
Bend, break and bleed to feed the Boss;
Bend, break and bleed? Ah, damn it, NO!
Fight on, fight on; let's go, LET'S GO!

Honest, Bell, What Did Bruce Say?

About May 1, 1923, Malcolm Bruce, a Labor champion from Toronto, was invited to Glace Bay to address the miners in the Cape Breton area. In the course of his remarks Bruce was reported to have made some disrespectful reference to the British flag. It was peculiar, however, that these alleged remarks were noticed only by the representatives of the capitalist press. The Labor forces were prepared with hundreds of affidavits to prove that he had made no such remark. However, a capitalist government acting in sympathy with a capitalist press, issued a warrant for Bruce's arrest, and he was referred to as a "fugitive from justice." The local police failing to locate him, the provincial police were called in, and they made a ridiculous raid one night at the homes of Glace Bay citizens. At the home of Jim McLachlan they found a book on socialism, communism, or some such subject, and a great fuss was made over this. The fact is that they could have found the same book in the public library of any large town or city.

The incident attracted much attention about Glace Bay, and there was much discussion about Bruce's address and what he really did say. People who were in the audience were appealed to, and the burning question was: Just what remark did Bruce make? During the heat of the discussion this writer appealed to his friend, Tom Bell, editor of the Maritime Labor Herald, *in this manner:*

> Honest Bell, what did Bruce say
> On that memorable day?
> When in accents bold and loud
> He addressed that "vulgar crowd"
> Whom a clergyman of worth
> Calls the scum of all the earth.
> Why was this here action brought?
> Did he say them things or not?
> If he did, he ought to pay—
> Them was awful things to say.
> You was there and sitting near,

Tell me, Tom, what did you hear?
I ask ya like an honest Red,
What was it Bruce really said?

He must have used some awful words,
'Cause a lot of men with swords
Came from over Sydney way,
Marching down upon the Bay;
One had bright braid on his collar—
That guy owes me half a dollar
That I gave to buy him rum—
Lord! he used to be a bum!
Before he joined this policeman crew,
Nothing cheap he would not do.
But now—would you think the crown
Would send such men to hunt him down?
Of course I know Bruce is a Red—
I wonder what he really said?

Yes, these soldiers brave that day
Marched right out toward the Bay,
Came to Jim McLachlan's door,
Looked the whole place o'er and o'er,
And before the search was over,
Found a book with a red cover.

Ha! Here's evidence enough,
This here looks like dangerous stuff.
The captain hissed in someone's ear,
"Methinks that Malcolm Bruce is near."
So they hunted round some more,
'Neath the beds and 'hind the door;
Lord! They're sore on that poor Red—
I wonder what Bruce really said?

They tell me, Tom, they called on you,
Honest, Bell, now is that true?

'Twas after Bruce that they were sent,
But did you miss much when they went?
You're a sly one they do say,
And had your moonshine hid away.
I wouldn't trust that outfit much,
They would cut your throat for hooch—
Mostly all a bunch of bums
Armstrong picked up 'round the slums;
And I've heard some talk about
How Sydney wants to clean them out.
A good idea, Tom, I would say,
Send them some pay-night to the Bay.

The Hair-Breadth Escape
of Red Malcolm Bruce
(Very thrilling)

The charge was on a certain day
Somewhere 'round the first of May,
One Malcolm Bruce, a dangerous Red,
"Riz up," and someone said he said
As how he hoped to see the day
When the red flag would lead the way,
Proclaiming with its every wave
Emancipation of the slave.
Now, some there were about the hall
Who did not like that talk at all;
And who they were you well may guess—
Reporters for the highbrow press—
Men of the so-called better classes
Who hold themselves above the masses,
And who, like tattle-tales at school,
Are godly as the golden rule.
So these good men indignantly
Reported to the powers that be,
And word was sent throughout creation
To watch at every railway station.
"Inform all police," the powers said,
"We got to get this dangerous Red
Who openly defies the laws
And dares to help the workers' cause."

But strange, this man so hunted down,
Was hanging 'round about the town
From Thursday night 'til some time Monday,
Cool as any walnut sundae;
Nor did he hurry to depart,
Methinks some cops are "red" at heart
And generously could find excuse
To walk away from Malcolm Bruce.

So Bruce departed from the Bay,
Just spoke his piece and went away.
When we heard of him again
He was on a west-bound train.
Later, home, amidst applause,
He was fighting labor's cause,
While papers raved and raised the deuce,
'Twas thus away fled Malcolm Bruce.
To prove he didn't run away,
He's back again now at the Bay—
Walks right into our A.B.—
"Were you looking round for me?
By happy chance it reached my ear
That I was being sought for here;
And, keen respecter of the laws,
I hurried back to learn the cause."

Tell My Friend the Prison Warden I Hadn't Time to Call

(Sung by Malcolm Bruce)

Bruce's trial, or hearing, was almost laughable. The representatives of the capitalist press, summoned to substantiate their previous reports, now presented a pitiful sight. They labored to shift responsibility from one to another, and their evidence consisted of a mess of "I heard that he heard," and "He heard that I heard," until the magistrate threw up his hands and the next day dismissed the case altogether. It was a great victory for Bruce, and representing the labor press at the hearing, we reported the case in this manner:

Dear Bell: I will not ask for space
To cover such a feeble case,
Nor should I take the readers' time
To bore them with my roughneck rhyme;
A few good laughs and I am done—
Oh, Tom, me boy, ain't we got fun?
You tell them all about the law,
Leave me alone to laugh haw-haw.
Six men from different parts of town,
All summoned, mind you, by the crown,
Stood up, and each one swore in turn
As how he hoped some day to burn,
If on that Sunday in the hall
He heard Bruce say "them things" at all.
I marked the smile on every face—
The crown was building quite a case?

One witness don't remember where
He really was—but he was there—
Could not remember every word,
But someone said he overheard
That someone said he knew a man—
'Twas thus the story wildly ran
Till we were dizzy in the head

From "someone said that someone said."
I'll tell you, Tom, what someone said—
"We've got to get this dangerous Red;
Everything is working nice—
Cut him down at any price.
Besco has too much at stake—
Horrors! if the slaves awake!
Make some pretext, find some excuse—
We got to silence Malcolm Bruce."

But, bon voyage, Malcolm, on your way,
We hope you come another day,
And Malcolm, if you come again,
We won't invite you to the pen,
Or take such rare exceeding pains
To wrap you up in prison chains;
When next you speak it well might be
On eastern hospitality.
Alas, alas, our island fame—
I weep o'er old Cape Breton's shame.

Hey, Jim and Dan

The year 1923 was a stormy one for labor and labor's champions. Hardly was the Bruce incident closed when the steel strike came on, followed quickly by the sympathetic strike of the miners. The Cape Breton industrial centers were overrun by soldiers, provincial police and other invaders, which greatly aggravated the condition. I make the statement here, and will undertake to prove it, that these provincial police did assault innocent people who were not strikers, and as my statement is probably not sufficient, I refer the reader to the findings of the Royal Commission that sat in the city of Sydney. A railway employee, who was not a striker, testified under oath before that commission to having been beaten or assaulted by these so-called police. Yet when Jim McLachlan and Dan Livingstone published these facts, they were arrested for what was at first called "spreading false news." The same news was spread by everybody—the press of the province featured it. It was chiefly through the medium of the press that the information became general. If one citizen was guilty, all citizens were guilty. Yet, of thousands that discussed the incident, only two were arrested, Dan Livingstone and Jim McLachlan. The ridiculous charge of "spreading false news" was inspiring. How can anyone guarantee the absolute accuracy of news? We depend largely on the press. How do we know that there was an earthquake in Japan? How do we know old King Tut is dead? Spreading false news? We may be guilty of it every day. But it happened in this case that the news was not false.

Hey, Jim and Dan, we are coming too,
For spreading news the same as you;
We talked about these holy ones
And how they hid behind their guns;
Yes, right up in the grocery store
We talked the matter o'er and o'er,
One fellow told us what he saw,
But I suppose he broke the law.

Say, Jim, you know the widow Hughes
And how she loves a bit of news—

It will take more laws I fear than one
To ever stop the widow's tongue.
The same as me, the same as you,
She can't swear anything is true,
But, true or false, she will have the news—
Make room up there for widow Hughes.

Let's make the company refined—
It happens we recall to mind
That it was in the highbrow press
We read of all this dirty mess;
When Armstrong sent his hoboes down
To take possession of the town;
So if there's room up there for more,
We will send you up an editor.

What d'ya think, hey? Jim and Dan,
The boys are with you to a man,
And from their talk, Jim, I can tell
That everyone is red as hell.
Inform O'Hearn that Sunday morn
At least ten thousand reds were born,
And if he don't decide to free ya,
Maybe we'll be up to see ya.

Away False Teachings of My Youth

At the McLachlan trial in Halifax, the crown prosecutor said that it did not matter whether the statements published by the accused were true or not, that sometimes it was against the law to tell the truth. Right there perished all hope of justice. How are we to know which truths are against the law? A conscientious witness might well hesitate to tell the truth. Some truths are against the law. What truths? With truth goes justice, and the hope of justice. The oath is: "Do you solemnly swear to tell the truth, the whole truth, and nothing but the truth?" How can one tell the whole truth when some truths are against the law? Search me!

"Speak the truth and speak it ever; cost it what it will."— Extract from elementary schoolbook.

Away, false teachings of my youth,
It's now a crime to speak the truth;
This man of law has so decreed
That it's a base and foul deed
Well meriting the dungeon cell
For anyone to boldly tell.
Yes it's a crime for me or you
To state a thing we know is true.

Thank God, I'm getting old and grey,
I'd hoped to never see the day
This tortured world would recognize
This modern champion of lies.
What would our poor old mothers say?
Which one of us forgets the day
She urged upon our tender youth
To love, uphold and speak the truth?

The quality of guilt depends—
Now, truth about the rich man's friends,
Or any of the tribe about their tools—
A bold exposure of their acts,
A fearless statement of the facts,

May summon up a gallows grim
Or hang the prison chains on him.

So, let us warn the nation's youth
That it's a crime to speak the truth;
They make the law to fit the case,
To lead McLachlan to disgrace.
So crucify him on a cross
Because he dared to sass the Boss,
Because he had the guts to tell
The company to go to hell.

Merry Christmas to You, Jim

I have always insisted that there was nothing smart or clever in writing a rhyme or expressing one's thoughts in verse. Some people have referred to this action as a gift, but I have always regarded it as an affliction. Certain it is that when I get the itch to write in this manner I may as well submit to the urge at once as try to avoid the effort. Lines, lines, lines will come pouring into your head, and your fingers will begin itching to get hold of a pencil, while the devil or some of his imps will keep hissing in your ear, "That's a good line, and this, and this, and this." No mental effort is required, the only effort is physical, to get the stuff down on paper as it comes clicking into your head from the devil knows where. It is useless to try and change the line of thought by occupying your mind otherwise—while the stuff keeps pouring in, your brain will entertain nothing else. As far as mental effort or planning goes, I may say that stories and bits of verse credited to me were not written or composed by me at all—they were hissed into my head by the fairies or some other invisible agents.

Jim McLachlan spent Christmas of 1923 in prison, and I spent Christmas night of that year in a flop-house in another part of the country. Because accommodations were so poor, and perhaps because I had no supper, I could not sleep, and while I was in this uncomfortable position the fairies attacked me: "Merry Christmas to you, Jim; Merry Christmas to you, Jim; In your prison dungeon dim; In your prison dungeon dim," came pouring into my head as clearly as if someone was speaking in the room. I realized from past experience that I had to do my stuff, but I was handicapped. There was no electric or gas light in the room and only an old-fashioned lamp was available. I found a match and pencil, but did not have a scrap of paper. "Write it on the wall, write it on the wall," commanded the fairies, pausing in their dictation. That's what I did—wrote the following lines on the smooth board unpainted wall of the flop-house. The lines are probably there still, if the flop-house is.

> *Merry Christmas to you, Jim,*
> *In your prison dungeon dim....*

Merry Christmas to you, Jim,
In your prison dungeon dim;
What although the bars are cold,
They have sheltered hearts of gold,
Fit companions they for you—
Steel is strong and steel is true.
Ah, better, yes with you to stand
Than humbly lick a tyrant's hand,
Like slaves and traitors to the cause
Who pawn their souls for men's applause;
The steel were truer friend than him—
Merry Christmas to you, Jim.

The meanest, vilest dungeon hole
Can never stain an honest soul,
And prison stripes can't dim your star,
It's not where you are, but what you are.
Persecute you all they can,
But, Jim McLachlan, you're a man,
And by the God whom I adore,
I'd rather pace a prison floor
And sleep in dungeons dark and cold
Than sell my soul for Besco's gold;
His masters must be proud of him—
Merry Christmas to you, Jim.

The mines are as they have ever been,
Kids are starving 'round Sixteen—
Ah, but blessed are the meek,
Blessed with two shifts a week.
Paper buncombe is the same,
But now they don't know who to blame.
Before you went and broke the laws,
Jim McLachlan was the cause
Of all the sin, distress and crime
That might occur in modern time,
But now they can't blame it on him—
Merry Christmas to you, Jim.

The Wearing of the Red

I walked up-street this morning.
And it being May Day
I wore a crimson ribbon
You could see a mile away.
Most folks smiled in sympathy,
Others shook their heads,
And some just showed their ignorance
And terror of the Red.
But I smiled at those in pity—
A smile of lofty scorn
Some men are slaves by circumstance—
And some for slaves were born.

Young lady with ambitions
To shine in "sassiety"
Says she, "I want to shine my shoes,
Will you give that rag to me?"
Poor simple little pin-head.
Oh, God, you owe her brains!
I just bowed to her politely,
And I left her in her chains.
She thinks she is a highbrow,
Above the working mass,
And to sneer at workers' emblems
Is a way to show her class.

Tho' her father and his fathers
All were working men,
She wants to play aristocrat,
And to discredit them.
The hand that rocked her cradle
Is far beneath her now;
The hand that toiled to shelter her,
The hand that held the plow:
Poor silly little infant—
Will you never come to know?

If it were not for the workers
You'd have starved long ago?

Yet they call us trouble makers.
I never shook my head,
And I never said, "You quitters,
You ought to wear the Red."
I leave them their opinions,
But, by God, they'll leave me mine,
I am choosing my own colors,
And I'll wear them every time—
On every such occasion
Will that banner be unfurled—
A tribute to the workers:
To the men who feed the world!

*(Written on May 1st, 1924, between the hours of two and
five minutes past two, p.m.)*

To Forman Waye

During the dull period this winter, the months particularly of January and February, one entertaining way of passing the time was to get the daily press and read reports from the House of Assembly, then in session. Labor was represented by Messrs. Waye, Morrison and Steele, and these three men, true to their pre-election pledges, utilized every opportunity to bring the cause of Labor to the fore and to discredit the government, their recognized enemy. It would be silly to expect that these three men in a hopeless minority could introduce or carry any legislation favourable to their cause.

The eloquent and brilliant speech of Forman Waye when he attacked the Attorney-General will be long remembered by all parties. In the course of this address Waye congratulated Mr. O'Hearn on the telegram that he (O'Hearn) received from Roy Wolvin after McLachlan's conviction. This telegram suggested where the Attorney-General was taking his instructions from. Referring to the provincial police and discussing the charge that they were drunk when they rode down the citizens of Sydney, Waye said that "it would indeed be in keeping with the training of a dashing captain of infantry to give his men a stiff shot of rum before leading them to the attack." He considered it probable that they were drunk on that occasion. Dealing with a traitor, one Richardson from Sydney, Waye referred to him as "A Farmer member from a Labor constituency supporting a Liberal government."

Perhaps the writer will be permitted to introduce here a rhyme he wrote during the period referred to, which is in appreciation of Forman Waye and his work. It is not my habit to write personal poems, and I am not much given over to hero worship as was proven on one occasion when I was asked to write some complimentary junk about a certain Prince. I told the newspaper people on that occasion that my poems were not for sale by the yard, that silly demonstrations did not impress me, and that when I was not impressed I could not write, whether I had the inclination or otherwise. This was further proved on that occasion. I was impressed by the honest efforts of Forman Waye and I felt that if my humble ef-

forts would tend to show appreciation, they were at his disposal.

Let old Cape Breton stand today
And cheer her champion, Forman Waye,
Who bravely stood, hemmed in by foes,
Who all undaunted nobly rose
And hurled his challenge, hissing hot,
And for two hours steady fought,
Who voiced the ringing charge we sent
Against a rotten government.

God bless your red head, Forman Waye,
You spoke your piece, you had your say;
I doubt if I could do as well,
You told them just what I would tell.
If you ever need a vote or two,
Waye, I'll stump the mines for you.
Lord, I'm a happy child today—
You took their trenches, Forman Waye.

We have always found who'er we sent
To serve us in the government,
Before he went had much to say,
But lost his message on the way,
And when the hour came to strike,
Was mild, polite and humble like,
And long before the session's end,
Our enemy would be his friend.

But Forman Waye, now you're a boy
To fill a voter's heart with joy;
You don't forget whose cause you serve,
You've honesty and brains and nerve;
They can't use you to serve their ends,
You don't forget your working friends,
You take the message straight and true;
Forman Waye, we're proud of you.

Tell me, Forman, one thing more
Was O'Hearn very sore,
When you cracked the whip at him?
Did this enemy of Jim—
Did he crouch, and crawl and whine?
Did he? Honest, that was fine!
McLachlan is avenged, I'll swear,
Gosh, I'd like to have been there!

Send the Bill to Besco

Your bill for those toy soldiers was received, oh, Mr.
    King,
But does that few odd thousand cover everything
From the time of the invasion till the time they went
    away—
Is just three hundred thousand all we have to pay
For all their pretty uniforms, their horses and their
    feed?
My land, these peace-time soldiers are really cheap,
    indeed!
But it grieves us to inform you we're a little bit hard
    pressed,
And we have an empty feeling in the region of our
    vest.

Yet we hasten to assure you, we will place your bill
    on file;
We have another like it that has been there for quite
    awhile—
Another bill for soldiers sent us long ago;
We hope you will forgive us if we seem a little slow,
But in fact, my dear MacKenzie, times are dull with me
And the reason for this dullness is not hard to see.
Anyone in Canada, I'm sure, will say the same:
Our leaders lack ability; our government's to blame
For keeping idle soldiers who pose and bum around,
Instead of handing them a hoe to cultivate the
    ground,
Generals and colonels who loaf and eat their fill,
And when it comes to paying, you send us down the
    bill.
We would gladly do our very best to help you out,
    you know,
But we're sorry to inform you that our funds are kind
    of low.
Too bad those pretty soldiers should suffer any need,

They are really ornamental but we've other men to
      feed—
Yes, and little children—hungry women, too—
After we have paid that bill we will send the change
      to you.

In the meantime, a suggestion we would offer you:
If you sent this bill to Besco perhaps they would see
      you thru.
Yes, get a line on Wolvin and see if he will agree
To pay you for protection of his sacred property.
You heard him wail a year ago, his plant was being
      wrecked,
We did not ask protection—we have nothing to
      protect!
Nor have we any money, times are always hard
Besco owns this country, let them pay this Royal
      Guard,
Sorry to annoy you about this modest little sum
But we are jolly glad to tell you Besco's on the bum—
So I fear this little item will have to wait a while:
But we hasten to assure you we will place your bill
      on file.

Ain't it something awful how long some bills will
      run?
I remain,
        yours most sincerely,
                Dan Willie Morrison.

Give Us A Fighting Man

Here's a new song for you Fellers. If some of the local musicians would write music for this we might have something to sing at the next bouts. I don't claim that it is much of a song, yet it is as good as "Barney Google" or "Yes, We have no bananas." The writers of those successes I am informed made millions of dollars and "here's me" with six bits in my pocket. Is it any wonder that I am a Red?

If all the fighters we pay to see,
Must be brought here from the west,
I'll tell 'ya Freddy and Hughie Dan,
The kind we like the best.
It's a smiling cuss,
Who will stand and slug
Take and give a rap on the mug.
We like 'em rough and tough and clean
But never yellow or sore or mean.
Give us a man who will fight like Hell
And we'll give you the gold
To pay him well.

Chorus
Give us a fighting man,
With a wallop in either hand.
Not a waltzing fairy that shimmy dances
Polkas and Two-steps and snorts and prances.
We are easy pleased but we do hate that.
You never know where the critter's at.
You blink and wonder which way he ran.
Lord, but we love a fighting man.

We liked you Joe, Kid Wheeler,
And we liked you Irven too,
And we figure this Roy Mitchell,
Will pretty nearly do.
We don't care if you're beaten, Kid.

As long as you made a fight.
We'll take you up and wash your wounds
And nurse you through the night.
There ain't no one can always win,
Just do the best you can.
And you'll be liked in this man's town,
If you're a fighting man.

For old Cape Breton has had her fighting
In many a bloody ring.
She fought Kid Strike and Kid Hard-Times,
And Old Kid Everything.
It's not her style to stand and brag
Over the titles she got.
She's taken some awful lickings. Yes!
But damn it she always fought.
And when her next big battle comes,
She'll do the best she can.
And she'll welcome you, kid, and use you right.
If you're a fighting man.

"Go West, Young Man, Go West"

I was never very proud, indeed I was somewhat a-shamed, of the following rhyme which was written while I was in flight from the starving sections of the extreme eastern part of industrial Canada in the year 1925. In justice to myself I might state, however, that this farewell was written under certain handicaps while I had to keep one jump ahead of the conductor on the night train out of Sydney.

However, when that official finally caught up with me, he proved to be a good fellow who knew me. He shared the contents of his lunch can with me and let me ride free to the end of his run.

The winter winds are bleak and drear,
Methinks I better move from here;
Fly, fly, Old Timer, fly away
Before that dark December day
When gloom descends upon the town
And when the mines are all shut down,
When idle workers walk the street—
Up, Up, Old Timer, work your feet.
Hark ye the hungry people's cries,
The birds have left (and birds are wise)
Were naught but wisdom now methinks
To leave the ship before she sinks.

What comes? This shadow o'er my mind
For those I love and leave behind,
But some there are I cannot like—
I hopes you perish, Ike McIke.*
I don't forget our little clash,
I hopes the "pluck-me"** stops your hash;
Beware the evil eye of me—
I'll have revenge, you wait and see.

I know not whether north or south
Or east or west I'll roam,

But this I know, the night is dark
And I am far from home;
And creditors, dear creditors,
Don't think I mean you wrong,
If you wake up some morning
And find that I am gone.
Yes, I know that you are short
Just the same as I,
But I'll pay you, yes, I'll pay you
In the sweet by and by.

* *Ike McIke: Contemporary writer in the local press.*
** *Pluck-me: General store operated by the workers' employers.*

Cape Breton's Curse, Adieu, Adieu

During the strike in the Nova Scotia coalfields, a high official of the company stated that the strike would not last long because, as he expressed it, "The miners couldn't stand the gaff!" This was a slur that caused much comment. This man and his associates owned the company stores, or "Pluck-Me's," and the remark was obviously a threat to starve the miners into submission. Some time later it was announced in the press that the big coal corporation was in the receiver's hands, but this was probably a manoeuvre to freeze out some shareholders or attract new capital. The process was called "reorganization," and the same outfit bloomed again under another name. However, anything that suggested embarrassment for the big-shots was welcome news to this old radical, who rushed to his typewriter and, without ever lifting his nose, tore off the following lines, which he offers as real classical.

The Bosses couldn't stand the gaff—
Oh, let me write their epitaph!
Let's see, now—how should I begin?
Here lies a monster, born of sin,
Of sin, corruption, fraud, and worse—
Adieu, adieu, Cape Breton's curse.

Since that black day when first your hand
Grasped in its evil clutch our land,
Like some fat leech you played your part
To suck the life-blood from our heart,
Bred famine, riot, murder too—
Cape Breton's curse, adieu, adieu.

'Twas no avenger laid you low,
Your end was painful, sure and slow;
Ah, filthy monster, now confess,
You died of your own rottenness.
May Satan's imps attend your hearse—
Adieu, adieu, Cape Breton's curse.

"I Charge You, British Workers"

I charge you, British Workers, stand steady in this
    fight;
At last a chance is given you to fight for your own
    right.
Too long you fought for tinsel kings and capitalist
    laws
Who would not up and strike one blow in this, a
    worthy cause?
On many bloody battlefields the British fought like
    brothers.
Fight now as staunchly for yourselves as when you
    did for others.
What Shelley told your fathers, today I'm telling you,
"Remember you are many. Remember they are few."

Every red spot on the map, beneath the setting sun,
In Christian or in heathen land, the British Workers
    won.
And yet the British Worker lacks land, lacks work,
    lacks bread.
Yes, the British Worker lacks a place to lay his head.
The lands he won belong to kings and capitalists fat,
And earls and dukes and idle bums and lord gods
    this and that;
All parasites who boasted of how the slaves could
    fight,
Now rally, men, the time is here to show them they
    were right.

Every creature fed in Britain, the British Worker fed,
In every worthy action the British Worker led.
When shots flew fast in battle, 'twas workers manned
    the gun.
What? Give ye up so tamely what ye so bravely won?
It's yours. Come take it, comrades. The Mine, The
    Farm, The Soil,

Are all the fruits of labor, you won them with your
    toil.
The drones still fatten on you, while you still sweat
    and strive,
Awake, awake, my comrades, it's time to clean the
    hive.

For nearly twenty centuries have British Workers
    fought,
It's only fair to question now, what they ever got?
They got a lousy blanket and a shilling perhaps as
    pay.
And some fool remarks about GLORY when their
    limbs were shot away.
They got shell shock and blindness and a belly full of
    brass.
And when a "blessed peace" returned, each one was
    made a slave.
They fought for LAND and got it, yes, six feet for a
    grave.

I charge you, British Workers, stand steady in this
    fray.
As you so often fought before, so fight ye all today.
Rally 'neath your banner Red and smite and smite
    and smite.
This is no senile kingly whim, no capitalist fight.
You strike for wife and baby, for freedom and for
    home.
The other was the masters' fight, this one is your
    own.
Ah! could you for a moment but realize your might.
I charge you, British Workers, stand steady in this
    fight.

The Parasites

In every contest between Capital and Labor, I am with Labor and against Capital first, last, and all the time. And if you ask me what percentage of the actual product of labor capital should receive, I cry loudly, "None, damn it, none!" But be assured that I class all worthy productive or creative effort as labor, and summed up, my contention simply is that any person who does not work at all, should not eat at all, excepting of course invalids and children.

Met a fellow the other day,
As I was roaming along the way,
They called him a radical, socialist, red,
Lowbrowed wretch who had been misled.
He talked of the workers, talked of their cause,
Talked of the country, talked of its laws—
An old young man, though tattered and frayed,
He was wise to the way the game was played;
None of your whiskered, bomb-throwing kind,
He had some ideas at large in his mind;
Dreamed of a day when his kind would be free—
Here's some of the line he handed to me:

Imagine a world of a hundred men,
And suppose they were workers every one;
God gave us the soil, God gives us the rain,
And for little work God gives us the grain.
A hundred cry "Clothing!" a hundred cry "Meat!"
But fifty work and a hundred eat.
If the idle half and their fathers and mothers
Would all go to work, they'd be little work-brothers,
But Jones and Smith and Green and Brown
Do all the work, while the rest stand round.
What of the other fifty per cent?
Jones and company pay them rent;
But 'twas Jones and company built the whole town—
I'm ashamed of you, Jones and Green and Brown.

Clara Vere de Vere's grandpa
Was a better thief than your grandma;
There goes Clara in her car,
She's kind to the poor as she drives up-street,
If the poor don't work, Clara don't eat.
Who is that with her? Reggie Deluxe,
His old man was a prince of crooks—
Two helpless, hopeless, pitiful tools,
Though they toured the world and been through
    the schools;
Producing nothing, everything bought—
The day they die the world will lose naught.
Your little bootblack, untutored, untaught,
He has use in the world, while these others have
    not.

From Clara's shoes to her new French gown,
Not a thing does Clara own;
Madame Dupre makes her suits,
Paris workmen build her boots;
Her hats are made by working girls,
Her maid Nanette combs out her curls,
This same Nanette puts on her clothes
And pedicures her little toes.
Her lunch is served by 'Enry Awes,
She hustles for neither meat nor sauce,
But discusses the servant problem—
"Really, it's hard to bother with them,
This most annoying servant class,"
She remarks to Mrs. Van Dam Ass.

Beasts in the jungle, bums on the street,
All must hustle that they may eat;
Fish in the sea and birds in the air,
Must hunt around for a living fare.
Nature for naught has naught to give—
You have to work if you want to live;

But Clara and her useless kin
Neither sow nor do they spin,
For they have gold—oh, they don't need to—
Yet gold will neither clothe nor feed you.
The world is nicely arranged for them
Who live by the efforts of other men—
Live by the sweat of the poor and weak,
Then marvel that men turn bolshevik.

Call me a socialist, radical, red,
Turning to me the old guy said,
"A lazy, disinterested, radical dub,
I may be all that, but I rustle my grub;
And I'm taking no job in your factory or mine,
I'm off the stuff, it's out of my line;
But I never beg and I never steal,
I do an odd job when I want a meal.
Maybe you cannot see it my way,
But that's all I get if I work all day.
If the deal was square, I'd do my bit,
If all would work, I'd never quit;
But I'm keeping no Claras—aw, what's the use?
It's her kind cry 'production'
                              — well, let 'em produce."

Mon Père

My father was a carpenter
Who worked hard every day,
His back was bowed, his hands were hard,
His locks were thin and gray.
That was many years ago—
The Locals then were small,
And every man who met the boss
Would touch his hat and crawl.
But father had a rebel's heart,
And often he told me
Of how he hoped to see the day
When workers would be free.

Now, father was no prophet,
Nor am I a prophet's son,
But today it is apparent
That the bosses' day is done.
When I hear the mighty unions
Proclaim the rights of man,
And I see the groups endorsing
The co-operative plan;
When no more will rank injustice,
Sustained by greed and lies,
March boldly down the highway
Garbed as "free enterprise."

There are those who name this racket
Where they hold the winning hands
Through control of all resources
And through title to the lands;
Where gold's the mighty master
With which goods are bought and sold,
Where the slaves are empty-handed
And the lords have all the gold.
With the cards stacked so pretty,

Would the sucker then be wise
To play this bosses' racket
That he calls "free enterprise"?

No, my brothers, shun the tempter—
The whole setup is a steal;
Fight and work for social justice—
Close the ranks for a new deal.
Down with hunger, slum, depressions,
Heed the swelling socialist call;
Why should you and yours be hungry
When there's plenty here for all?
What Shelley told your fathers,
Today I am telling you—
Remember you are many—
Remember they are few!

Part 2

Autobiography
or
"A Biography of
Oswald Donald 'Dawn' Fraser
by An Observer"

A Biography of Oswald Donald "Dawn" Fraser, by An Observer

ON JULY FIRST IN THE YEAR 1888 there was
born in the town of Antigonish, Nova Scotia, to Mr.
and Mrs. Simon Fraser a male child, and it was soon
evident to observers that this new citizen was going
to develop into a disagreeable, aggressive addition to
the world's population.

For as soon as the infant's eyes were open and he
glanced up into the world, he frowned hideously and
let out a howl evidently in protest to being born.
Some days later when a rather romantic maiden
aunt took him to church to be named, she chose the
name of Oswald and it is on record that at this mis-
take the child howled even louder.

Later, when he had returned to its modest home
and the name Oswald was being discussed, the child
babbled some baby talk, like, "Goo Goo Boola Camera
Hascha." This interruption was ignored by all
present except the child's uncle Archie Chisholm who
was a "braw Scot" and something of a Gaelic scholar.
This gentleman insisted that the wee laddie had
spoken in the Gaelic tongue and what it uttered was,
"Oswald. That's a hell of a name to tag on a wee help-
less Scotchman."

And it soon developed that few in that atmosphere
could get their Scotch tongues around the word Os-
wald. The nearest most of them could come to it was
Arse-well. However, with Christian patience the
child bore the disgrace of not carrying one of the pop-
ular Scottish names of John, Duncan, Dougald, or
Alex. Nearly all Scottish children were called after
their father, mother or grandparents.

As the boy developed to school age it was soon evi-
dent that he possessed an inquiring but not a sub-
missive mind. If he had one virtue it was his great
love of truth. This did not necessarily arise from any
moral sense, but it seemed that he had a terror of be-
ing deceived and in his opinion even his schoolteach-

ers were trying to deceive him. An instance of this: There was a school book called *The Health Reader*. On one page under question, "Ought A Boy To Use Tobacco." We were assured that such a habit stunted the growth and if we wanted to develop big and strong we should avoid the poison weed. But the contradiction to this was right before our eyes; at the next desk sat big Donald Chisholm. He was big and very well developed. He could beat any boy in the school, yet he smoked and chewed tobacco at every opportunity. And nearby sat Duncan McDonald whose father had a store where he could steal enough tobacco to keep him and his pals supplied at all times. Duncan was also big and strong and a terror on the football field.

Now, here was falsehood flung right in our faces, and it made young Fraser lose confidence in his teachers and others who took the same attitude. Why were adults trying to fool us? There was a small book called *A Brief History of England*. It gave a review of the Chinese Opium War, which did not occur in the darker ages but in the reign of Queen Victoria probably about the year 1850. This book revealed or confessed that British merchant ships had been smuggling opium into China from India. The boy emperor of China wished to stop this traffic, which was making dope slaves of his people. He seized one British opium-laden ship.

England at once declared war. Beat the Chinese in battle, stole the island of Hong Kong and forced the Chinese to open three more ports for them to peddle their drug. Now that is substantially what we read in the schoolbook, but a short time later we were singing some patriotic song about how "England's flag has always stood for justice." Now, when a young person finds such deceptions in his youth and in the schoolroom, is it remarkable if he is suspicious of anything that is told to him or taught to him in later years? And if such exposures are considered disloyal this writer is in good company.

Walter Scott, referring to Pitt, the great English statesman, wrote,

> "He, who an outraged heaven gave
> For England's sins, an early grave."

I, AN OBSERVER, who dictated the first part of this history find it hard to continue with accuracy. I get mixed up with the "He" and the "I," so I have decided to seek out Mr. Fraser who does not live far from me, and ask him to continue the big story, which follows.

I have had only an ordinary education. I did creep up as far as high school but did not graduate. What knowledge I have has been supplied by reading and travelling. Reading English literature at school I loved MacAulay's *Lays of Ancient Rome* but hated all the Greek stuff about Homer, the Heathen gods and the "hero Sirius who was sired by the God Zeus and whose mother was a white swan." This stuff, I understand, is considered classical but it is all just trashy lies to me.

I have lived for a number of years in the United States and have a certificate in pharmacy from the state of Massachusetts. Never liked the profession. In those days very long hours and very little pay. I had an urge to wander, see what I could see and learn what I could learn. Among my tons of reading down through the years I was attracted to the stories of Jack London who wrote much of the jungles and the free wandering life of the hobo. One day I collected the small amount of salary due me at the drugstore where I worked, put on my coat and hat and walked on to the railway station. There I bought a ticket for the nearest junction point, alighted there and walked away, away anywhere. I had a nice sense of freedom. No more regular duty, no more regular hours. It was summer time, but summer would not last. I was heading south like the birds. In my pockets were a safety razor, a toothbrush, soap and a tablet of writing paper, also a couple of stubs of lead pencil. At a pawn shop in a small town I exchanged my city clothes for a suit of overalls, a cap and a cheap sweater, and got a few dollars in the bargain. I walked and walked, out into the wilderness. That night I slept under a tree beside a little brook.

I could always entertain myself by repeating in my mind little verses in Rhyme. I know most of Service's stuff by heart. I also like Doctor Drummond's little stories in verse. Oscar Wilde's *Ballad of Reading Gaol.* The pad of paper I carried and the bits of pencil were originally intended as material for a diary. When I got hungry I would stop at some cheap restaurant for a lunch. Verses were constantly in my mind. I could supply some rhyme or proverb for nearly any experience that I met. If it were stormy or disagreeable I could soothe myself by repeating:

"But Roderick, though the tempest roar,
It may but gather and pass o'er."

I could also quote from the Koran:

"What Allah wills will be."

I was really religious and never missed my prayers morning or night.

I wandered through many states and when I needed money I went to work. One can always find work if he is not too fussy and really wants to work and is not lazy. I have picked spuds in the state of Maine, peaches in Maryland, was a bank clerk in Nova Scotia, worked in the coal mine, in the lumber woods, on construction jobs, in a sardine packing plant and for short times at other jobs and in each of those positions I learned more than I ever did at school. Did you ever know that a lawbreaker could serve the sentence of the court in a coal mine? Well? One night a bunch of us were in the bunkhouse of a logging camp. There was a big white fellow there from Pennsylvania, another white boy from British Columbia and a colored boy named Mappy Jones from somewhere. The two white men were discussing coal mining methods when Jones volunteered some information.

"Shut up, nigger," said the big boy from Pennsylvania. "What do you know about coal mining?"

"Ah did something you guys never did in a coal mine. Ah was taken off a freight train in Virginia for stealing a ride and I got six months. But I never served it in jail or any prison. I was put to work in Mr. Joe Brown's coal mine. The boss of the prison sold my labour to his friend Joe Brown."

"I told you to shut up, Nigger. Don't believe you ever worked in your life."

Jones looked at the other with teeth and eyes flashing.

"Do you think I'd take that if we were alone?"

"You got to take it," said the big guy.

"Yah. Maybe with all your white friends here," said Jones.

"You're not so much alone, Jones," several white men assured the colored boy who was the only Negro there. This lack of support cooled the big bully. The fact was Jones was popular in camp and the big guy was not.

What else did I learn in the jungle, you might like to know. Well, did you ever think that a man might be too good for a job? That happened to me.

During a business depression, not the one of '29 and the "hungry thirties," but away back in 1906. Like many others I was unemployed and if one answered an Ad in the newspaper there would be hundreds assembled to answer it. One morning I was lucky. The proprietors of a large and luxurious store which marketed Ladies' furs wanted a man to stand at the door, open the carriage door from which the fashionable ladies alighted, and wear a blue and gold monkey uniform with fancy cap advertising the firm's name.

As I said, I was lucky. There were not such a great many applicants and the few who were ahead of me evidently were unsatisfactory. So when my turn came to stand before a sharp-eyed prospective employer I had my case all ready. I had worked in a bank, in various local drug stores, on the ledgers for the big soap company, Lever Bros., makers of Rinso.

I had references in my pocket from these former employers etc., etc., etc.. The little man never interrupted me until I was nearly out of breath. Then when I was about to start all over again he said, "That will do, young man, you have convinced me that you are too good for this job."

"Oh sir, you would not blame me for that?"

"No, no. Certainly not. I would admire you for it. But do you expect me to entertain this mob every morning? Good day, young man."

"Damn smart little yankee," I murmured as I left the office. Now, I do not wish to be tiresome. I do not even know how much of the material is wanted or who wants it. All I know is that I had a phone call requesting it. So I will hurry to a conclusion.

THE FIRST GREAT WORLD WAR, 1914-1918, had commenced, and I was back in Boston. I had been turned down by the American Army and Navy on account of defective teeth. Now here was a queer condition. All employers had been warned not to employ anybody who was in the American Army draft. The army might need me later if the going got too tough, regardless of my dental condition. But I might starve before they called me. One day walking up Bromfield Street I saw a Canadian flag in a window with lots of war pictures and advertising. The Canadian Government had opened a recruiting office in that American city. I hopped right in, bummed a dollar from the very pleasant recruiting officer, telling him I needed a couple of shots of Rye to keep my courage up. I would pay him the dollar later in case I did not get killed. That same night I was on a train for Aldershot Camp, Nova Scotia. After training for a time in Canada we were moved to the west coast from where we finally sailed for Vladivostock, Siberia, in eastern Russia.

Some philosopher, I forgot just who, has written, "There is a divinity which shapes our ends, rough hew them as we may," meaning, I presume, that we do not always do what we intended to do or what we would like to do, because some circumstance pops up to make our wish or hope seem impossible.

Take my position when I enlisted in the United States. It was not any patriotic urge that prompted me. Army life or discipline did not attract me. There was a possibility I would be killed and also a suggestion by the newspapers of the day that I would be eaten. During those years of the Russian Revolution I had read of starvation in Russia and of people eating human flesh. Consider my position: The American Army and Navy had refused to consider me for service on account of defective teeth, but no employer was permitted to consider me either. The order was strict. Don't interfere with any men who have registered in the draft. We don't need Class B men now but we may need them at any time and we may never need them if the war comes to a quick end. But they did not invite me to dine and sleep at the army barracks. They were holding me in suspension, in reserve, and did not seem to care if I starved. I could not eat so I had to take a chance of being eaten. So I enlisted as already recorded. Now whether it was a divinity that forced me to this decision I do not know. Yet it proved to be the best break I ever got.

It was customary at Willows Camp in British Columbia and later at Gornisti Bay in Russia for the officers to arrange entertainments, known as "hook nights." Every soldier was urged by his officers to attempt to contribute to the show. If he could not sing, he had to dance, box, or even tell some funny story. If he failed to try for the honour of his company, he would not be punished or court marshaled, but he would be considered yellow and would be unpopular in his company ever after.

When I got my orders to do my bit I was at first stumped, but I went over to the gym, got a lead pencil and some paper and wrote some verses. It was the rainy season in the west and mud was thick and deep. I called my effort "The Mud Red Volunteers." I read or recited it that night and it was a howling hit. It must have been funny because they howled applause with every line. There were money prizes contributed by the officers and I won the pot. Merit being decided by which performer got the most applause when he was paraded before the audience at the conclusion of the show. There were many other hook nights after the first and my officers insisted that I write something for every show.

I will not comment further on the merit of what I wrote but I won the prize on every occasion until finally the other so-called artists refused to compete, saying that Fraser would get the prize anyway. There was no jealousy or ill feeling, the boys were good sports. We did not need money, we had no board to pay. So I spent my prize on vodka, shared the drink with those who would accept it, and said that if they liked my stuff, I would still try and write. But would accept no more prize money. And I was surprised as anybody with the stuff that came into my head. I could create characters that I never saw and spin yarns that were pure fiction. There was nothing smart about it. I did not have to think. That stuff would come into my head just as fast as if it was coming over the radio and I would have to write fast with the stub of a pencil to catch it as it flowed, each line would rhyme with the one preceding it and they would seem to carry the appropriate same number of words. For instance,

> I walked into a jungle
> Somewhere in the west.
> I walked into a jungle
> To give my dogs a rest

●

> If you can't say something good about me
> Please say something bad
> Lay on MacDuff, my hide is tough.
> I'll thank you for the Ad.

I do not know if a divinity was shaping my ends or whether the stuff was coming from Mars.

EVEN AFTER I WAS BACK in civil life and at home I was not very smart on the typewriter, and my gentle mother used to call my efforts "Tapping." I would be lost in the middle of some yarn and Mother would say, "Oh, stop that and come to lunch." But the stuff would be coming over even after I went to the table and I would leap up saying, "Oh, there is a good line," and back I would go to the machine. If some guests came in and my presence was needed I would appear, but the stuff would keep crowding into my head until it arrived at some intelligent conclusion.

I note that I am beginning to make mistakes in my typing, a sure sign that I am getting weary. I am not as young as I used to be, so I must conclude this effort as gracefully as I can.

My book published first in 1921—1000 volumes
Later enlarged under same title—2000 volumes.
Finally enlarged under *Narrative Verse*—2500 volumes.

They have been disposed of and I have none to offer now. I had a rather original way of marketing my books. When I found that they moved very slowly when left on consignment in local bookstores, I invaded homes with a briefcase full of books, asking the householder to permit me to leave the book. They paid nothing, promised nothing, signed nothing; please read a little of it. I would like your opinion. I am not sure whether it is any good or not. I will call again in a week or so with your permission and if it does not interest you, I will pick it up and thank you for your very kind cooperation.

I regret to state that I never received any favourable notice by the press of my native province. I have seen pictures in the local newspapers of the newly appointed dog catcher and of little Johnny Jones who passed his examination from the first grade into the second, but never have I seen it recorded that Dawn

Fraser was even alive. Perhaps they wished I was not. Perhaps I offended them with some of my observations. Oh, yes. There is one exception to this complaint.

When the first edition of my book appeared more than thirty years ago, the old *Halifax Chronicle* in a review of literature stated exactly this, I quote: "We would say offhand that Dawn Fraser writes as good verse as Service. We would call this Nova Scotia poet a Jim Tully in rhyme, an Edgar Guest with more guts and less Pollyanna-ism." I have heard, but am not sure, that it was a professor Logan of Dalhousie who dictated that comment. If it was and if the gentleman is still living, I am grateful to him.

And finally—I am a humble old fellow. I have not sought social distinction. If I had such ambitions I would not confess that I had been a hobo or had only an elementary education. It is my belief that everybody has some talent and it is a duty to try and develop it. I did not train to be a writer. The stuff was forced upon me. It kept crowding into my head and I had to expel it as surely as I had to exhale my breath. I claim to be a real democrat. I scorn titles and crowned heads. I dislike the word "Master" when applied to anybody except God Almighty. To hear anybody called "Excellency" or "My Lord" or "Your Grace" or "Your Highness" makes me smile. We all have our faults. Nobody is excellent, and those who assume those titles are no better than anybody else. As Kipling wrote,

> The colonel's lady
> And Judy O'Grady
> Are sisters under the skin.

And Robert Burns insisted that "A man was a man for all that." I have been told on occasions that I was "persona non grata." I have also been called a Red. Weak characters always consider that a clever way to win an argument. Call him a Red. But I am weary and must stop. I hope the above comments will be satisfactory to whoever requested them and I thank that party for being interested enough in me to make the request.

GOOD MORNING FRIENDS. Here I am again.

After I went to bed last night the stuff still kept crowding into my head and I had difficulty dismissing my mysterious informer. This morning, reviewing what I had written last night, I feel that some statements should be revised or elaborated upon.

Some readers may say, "This man Fraser suggests that the use of tobacco makes young people and children big and strong. Ha; Ha; we see the point. Fraser is writing in the interest of the big tobacco companies and he is being well paid to poison our children."

Money, money, money. Some people cannot get the charm of money out of their heads. I never intended to suggest that the tobacco they consumed nourished big Ronald or Duncan or that the lack of it weakened other young people. But it is possible that the association that went with the tobacco helped to strengthen and develop the big boys. These were perhaps more neglected at home and were allowed to wander after school hours and on holidays down to the old swimming hole, to chase the fire engine, out in the fresh air and eat like young savages at home. Their less fortunate weaker companions were more carefully disciplined. Had to come right home after school and apply themselves to study, about Homer and the ancient Gods who never existed. Greek mythology and all that nonsense. These poor victims had little exercise, not enough fresh air, poor appetites, probably wore eyeglasses at an early age and had soft flabby muscles. No wonder they were afraid of Big Duncan or Ronald. As to the scene in the schoolroom, of course I excuse the teacher. She was not free. She was an employee and had to preach what she was told to preach, and sing what she was told to sing. Honesty and truth today is a thing of the past.

I once conducted a column in a daily paper hoping

that I could (parade) some truths. But no. I had to be the slave of the owner of the paper. I had to write what he thought, not what I thought. Once a prominent citizen died. He (was) neither an angel or a demon, but other writers mourned and mooned over him. He would be missed forever. He could never be replaced etc., etc.

I needed something for my column that day, so I told some truths about the "late lamented." My employer called me on the carpet and he was raving mad. Relatives of the dead man were going to sue the paper, but they never did. I could prove what I had written to counteract the hypocricy in the other papers, but when I said to the Boss,

"What I wrote was the truth—"

"I don't care a damn whether it was the truth or not. I don't want it in my paper. It is bad for circulation." I was warned.

So acute is the money urge today that nearly all business is deception. Advertisers will insist that their product is the very best but is still the very cheapest. Now that presents a contradiction. The big soap promoters will declare that their product Soapso is positively perfect. But a short time later they will announce that Soapso has been improved. If it was perfect in the past, it could not be improved. Motor car dealers will sell old cars and declare that they are JUST LIKE NEW. I pause to laugh. It's all such a mess of lies.

My favourite philosopher is the one who said, "Money is the root of all evil"—and my favourite clown is the one who replied, "Well, give me plenty of the root, ha, ha. Am I not a funny guy?" I am also an admirer of Diogenes, the old boy who was wandering around in the dark some ages ago with a lighted lantern. When asked what he was seeking, he replied that he was looking for an honest man.

On one occasion amid a lot of citizens, I dared to declare that I did not want money and did not like money. This remark was greeted with hoots of derision. "Ha ha, I would hate to try him with a million dollars. Ha ha." "What would you do with a million dollars?" I wanted to know.

"Wine, women and song. Travel," they replied.

I have tried all those, I insisted. I have travelled until I was weary. I have drunk until I was sick. I have gambled until I lost what little money I ever had. I will not discuss women. Good ones are akin to angels and bad ones and gold diggers can be devils.

No, I do not seek money, popularity, fame or fortune. "The paths of glory lead but to the grave." I have met some wealthy people, but I never met a really happy one. It is doubtful if any of us were intended to be happy in this world, and it is stated that the happiest people ever observed were the slaves, coloured slaves, in the southern cotton fields who could keep singing all day as they toiled in the hot sun.

But cheer up. Perhaps we will all go to heaven or somewhere where we will be happy. Be assured,

"What Allah wills, will be."

Part 3

Echoes of World War One

The Mud-Red Volunteers

They told us that in Europe
The Huns were running wild,
Of little children murdered
And womanhood defiled;
That it was a real man's duty
To be active in the fray—
"Before it is too late!" they cried,
"Oh, men, enlist to-day!"
But we eyed our old job fondly,
As we slowly sipped our beer,
It was Hell we knew in Europe,
It was pretty soft right here.
Could we give up "thirty bucks" a week
And march off to the front,
Perhaps to die amidst the Huns
For "thirty bucks" a month?
Ah! 'twas then we saw our duty,
Like the noble things we were,
Soon on our way to Aldershot,
All singing, "Over There."
Oh! Aldershot, white-tented,
Cold, wet and beastly grim,
Where my courage was first dented
When someone screamed, "Fall In!"
Where I first met sergeant-majors,
Heard their wild Apache yell—
Midst the "Fall in, Fall out, Double quick!"
We have seen a bit of Hell;
Reveille's at six am, the sergeant-major's cue,
And then he starts in plenty
To tell you what to do.
Clean, Shine up—they drive you on
Like any bloody slave—
P. T., Fall in, Fall out again,
Nine seconds left to shave;
And you can't do this, you can't do that,

It's all against the rule;
We wanted to be heroes,
Not little kids at school;
We must keep away from Woman,
She's a real live pizen-snake,
Believe me, boys, I am thinking
Our M. O.* is a fake;
Did you get those hygiene stories,
And the pictures on the wall?
Say, I know a guy who knew a girl,
And he never died at all.
So our *esprit de corps* is waning,
All our pluck and interest too,
The only thing we see to fight
Is mud and Spanish "flu";
And we often dreaming wonder
Will the quarantine always last?
As we work like slaves at present,
Thinking sadly of the past.
They are taking us to Russia,
As soldiers of the King,
And if we see a Bolshevist,
We will shout, "You horrid thing!"
Or perhaps we will "shun" a dozen times
And double up our fist;
Then all "form fours" our very best,
And slap him on the wrist.

*** M. O.: Medical Officer**

My Tutor, the Professor of Stabbing

IN THE YEAR 1916 the Government became interested in my education and gave me a free course in the art of bayonet fighting. Previous to this I had enlisted in the army for what I understood was relief work and when I told the recruiting officer that, being a nurse and pharmacist, I felt that I would qualify as a stretcher bearer, ambulance man or in a dispensary, he was as usual enthusiastic and quite agreed with me.

Now understand please, I was not applying for a commission or soft snap. In my ignorance at that time I imagined that to be an officer one must really be a veteran of the Boer War, the Egyptian War or some other war, and that he must have at least a dozen notches on his rifle indicating that he was indeed a hard dog, and in his day had disposed of the lives of at least a dozen ordinary men. But regardless of promises or arrangements with the recruiting officer when I arrived in Canada, I was placed in the Infantry and when I protested I was told that this was merely a temporary arrangement and that a little later the government would build me a drugstore in No Man's Land. They even assured me that my store would be so conspiciously placed that it would be patronized by all the Allies and the Germans as well. But my ambitions were never realized and we were finally taken for training to Willows Camp, Victoria, B.C. Here they gave me a number as indeed one other government did on a previous occasion, they finally offered me a Lance-Corporal stripe; but I was not interested in stripes; in fact I was suspicious of them, the other Government referred to had given me quite a number of stripes. They also hung a lot of advertising matter on me, such as 260 Batt, Inf., etc., etc.

Our elementary training was hurried through and I was finally turned over to my tutor. Meet Sergeant English, professor of bayonet fighting, and imagine the field of his activities. A level plain devoid of grass or vegetation, what ballplayers and athletics refer to as a skin diamond. At one end of this area a series of upright posts with bars running along the entire top, and suspended from these bars a lot of swinging dummies made of sticks and rushes tied tightly together, the general dimensions of these dummies being about the same as a man's body. These inoffensive objects you are told by the professor are supposed to represent Germans, and your business there is to practice sticking a bayonet in them. In a preliminary lecture the professor assures you that you cannot be too dirty in bayonet fighting, your business is to get your man any way that you can. Now he would cry, At his throat; Long Point; damn it, put some pep in it; now again, I want you to grunt this time. Fraser, get that silly grin off your face, look fierce, look serious, look murderous, curse, swear; damn it, make it snappy. Charge together. High Port, come back here, you are like a lot of old women. Ah I wish the Royal Guards could see you. If the Kings Awn could see you? they would laugh, they would laugh, and you're Kanidians, Kanidians.

Then the professor would grab a rifle from one of us and show us how the Kings Awn would do it, and I must admit he was a real athlete and was good at it. He would stab that poor old bundle of sticks as gracefully as a society matron would carve a chicken. But that was the only thing he could do, he was of less than average intelligence, thought that an expert bayonet fighter was the finest thing in the world and that he was the most expert bayonet fighter in the world. He would click his heels together and pose in front of us and he could not understand why we refused to get enthusiastic over his example. Most of his scorn was directed at me as I was doubtless the least graceful of the bunch and certainly the least interested. On one occasion when I made a particularly feeble thrust at the imaginary German and returned to my place with the point of my bayonet trailing on the ground, the good professor became very scornful.

Man! Man! What are you doing? he groaned. I have not the least idea. I replied. No! No! I don't think you have, you'll be a soldier come twelve years, he answered.

The unutterable scorn in his voice, the look of disgust and sneering expression on his face, got my goat, and I said. Yet wait, the truth, I said nothing aloud. I had been in the Guard Room before; but what I said under my breath would be enough to annihilate the Royal Guards, the Kings Awn and the poor professor combined. Man! Man! I echoed him while my heart cried out for permission to speak. Man! Man! poor foolish man of the clouded intelligence, do you think I want to be what you are, to be what you take pride in being? An expert stabber of human beings, a professional trained killer, the thought that I should ever become expert appalled me.

Perhaps I was not in the habit of praying, at least not often enough, but I prayed then, prayed sincerely. Oh! Loving and Almighty God don't let me ever become what this man is trying to make of me: a trained killer, a professional destroyer of human bodies. I feel that I have enough to answer for, but if I cultivated this barbarous talent against the protests of my conscience, I might indeed despair of your mercy. Forgive this man, God, he knows no better, and help me God, because I do know better and am here a victim of circumstances. What may not be wrong for him is certainly wrong for me because my conscience and every sense that you gave me rebels at it.

That was my prayer and to this day it has been answered for, although I went overseas, I was never compelled to take advantage of my meager training at the school of Professor English. Now let all the gentlemen of the Military Camps say, he is a yellow rat, he has no guts, he is scared. Let me tell you, Oh Heroes with your pretty medals, I have been in just as tight corners as you ever were, and it was not in a trench or in wartime either, and I did not have to go to France to find these tight corners. Afraid to die?

Oh no, friends, not necessarily. Did you ever wish to die and could not? It is sometimes harder to live than to die.

> How often, Oh how often,
> I have wished that the ebbing tide
> Would bear me off on its bosom,
> O'er the ocean wild and wide.
> For my heart was heavy within me,
> And my brain was filled with care,
> And the burden which lay upon me,
> Seemed greater that I could bear.
> —Longfellow.

Beautiful words eh? Still I presume this is only another form of cowardice.

The Valets of the Mules

(Describing the loss of the S.S. RUSSIAN *in the Mediterranean Sea, January, 1917)*

We were mostly "lit" with booze
When we sailed from Newport News,
And the skipper that we signed with
Offered five pounds for the cruise.
We were bound—no matter where—
'Twas the war front over there;
No one liked to answer questions
And us valets didn't care.
Our cargo? Could you guess?
It was mostly mules and us—
Mules they had gathered near and far
For their awful game of war.
Us they had signed as simple tools
And as valets for the mules,
To serve their meals and make their bed,
Clean their rooms and hold their head.

'Twas December's dreary day
When we slowly steamed away—
Somewhere off an English port
Came two cruisers, our escort
Through the submarines and mines
Safely to the British lines.
Our escort, we thought, poor fools—
They were to escort the mules.
"Land those mules" was the command,
"Mules cost money—men be damned."

And we made the trip in peace,
Landed us somewhere in Greece;
Soon our cargo was ashore,
And we started back for more.
When we cleared for God's country,
Not a cruiser could we see;

We must play a lonely hand
Ere we reach old Yankee land.
"Save the mules," was the command,
"Mules cost money—men be damned."
And we sailed one early morn
Midst the fiercest thunder storm—
Thunder peals that screamed like shell,
Lightning that seemed from hell.
Out at sea twelve hours about,
When a U-boat picked us out—
Came a crash, an awful rip—
England lost another ship.
With a great wound in her side,
Bravely still she fought the tide,
'Til we swung the lifeboats free,
Grabbed a belt and put to sea—
Seas few lifeboats could have fought,
Some were lucky, some were not;
I saw them sink, one at a time,
Saw them swamped with friends of mine;
As I watched them disappear
I was crazed with hate and fear.
Fancied I could hear bells toll,
Then I damned the Kaiser's soul—
Damned the shark that claimed their prey,
Breathed a prayer and rowed away.

Later, off the coast of France,
We were picked up most by chance—
Battleship of Johnny Bull,
Called *H. M. S. Drypool*.
But you weary of my verse,
Anyway I've told the worst.
We were passed from hand to hand
Ere we sailed for Yankee land;
But all things end, so ends the cruise—
We were back at Newport News

With our five pounds, carried far,
We were back in Riley's Bar,
Drinking toasts to our old gals,
Drinking toasts to our lost pals;
Bore ourselves like men of wealth,
And we drank the Kaiser's health—
Drank the hope he'd rot in hell,
Likewise wished his family well;
Long before the night was done,
Damned the U-boats, every one;
They were murderers, devil's tools,
Killing poor valets of the mules.

Conscript Brown
or The Returned Man's Story

*There is a commandment of God, "Thou shalt not kill,"
and we are not at all convinced that war is an excuse for
breaking it. No, we are not convinced that because the
powers or the profiteers declare war, we should place a
rifle on our shoulder, march off to Timbuctoo and pump
lead into some native who is as innocent as ourselves.*

*We can find nothing in the Saviour's teachings to jus-
tify bloodshed. Indeed, on the very eve of the great trag-
edy, he rebuked Peter for an attack on the servant of the
high priest, notwithstanding the fact that the attack was
made in his own defense. Yet during the late war con-
scientious objectors were called cowards simply because
they hesitated to slaughter certain individuals who had
never injured them in any way.*

Perhaps you have heard me speak of Brown, who
    died at Stanislau,
In twenty years of service, there's the queerest case I
    saw,
And I have seen all kinds of soldiers, in barracks,
    tent and field,
The whitest men who ever fought, the yellowist who
    squealed.
'Twas back in 1917 I first laid eyes on Brown,
The M.S.A. was active and the police had run him
    down;
I am one who claims when that law passed, some
    body "pulled a bone"—
Such pale-faced, sickly kids as Brown should all be
    left at home.
Our company was made up most of men who done
    their bit,
And in a crowd like ours, a slacker didn't fit;
So no matter where we met him, round the canteen
    or in town,
The best he ever got from us was, "There goes
    Conscript Brown."

And we would ride him for his shallowness, his lack
    of nerve and pluck,
We never called him "Bud" or "Pal"— 'twas Con-
    script Brown that stuck;
But he took it half good-natured, though 'twas hardly
    meant that way,
Seemed a homesick, dreamy devil, with never much
    to say;
Till it struck me kind of sudden that a boy who could
    stand pat
Midst the sneers and jeers of hundreds, had a sort of
    nerve at that;
And I grew to like the beggar—used to often take his
    part—
Let them hit a kid who like it—I never had the heart.

So Brown and I grew chummy; Lord, he taught me
    half I know,
When it came to education—say, he'd make a monk
    look slow;
But he never made a soldier, though well-behaved
    and willing,
I say the way he moved around he was not meant for
    drilling;
At the miniature and in the butts he failed to qualify,
And as for bayonet fighting he couldn't harm a fly.
I have worked with him for hours, using all my time
    and skill—
That same night I heard him praying, something
    about "Thou shalt not kill."
And I often told him stories of hard knocks I took
    and gave,
Tried my best to stir him up, but he never thought
    me brave.
I remember one, a story of a fight we had in France,
Where I stabbed a half-starved Austrian who didn't
    have a chance;

His comment on that amazed me, thought my yarns
  had turned his head,
With an air like any parson, "That was murder, Bill,"
  he said;
And I could not argue him under, though I tried it
  there and then,
With nature's law and self-defence and all the laws
  of men.
The laws of men, he told me, with a kind of saintly
  nod,
Should always by subjected to the higher laws of
  God.
He had some queer religion, that's why he couldn't
  fight,
He wouldn't kill for any cause, he didn't think it
  right—
Was full of Bible stories, said God taught us to be
  meek,
And if a fellow slapped my face, to turn the other
  cheek.
Well, I had heard some stories, but that one took the
  pot,
And I thought of Africa and France and all the fights
  I fought;
Then my thoughts flew back to childhood, a kid on
  mother's knee—
Oh, far back in my mind it seemed she told those
  tales to me;
And later when in Sunday School the Bible class was
  taught,
I only half believed them, but they made me think a
  lot.
And I wondered really why men fought, the strong
  against the weak,
I knew there would never be a war if all men turned
  their cheek,
I thought of Liege and Rheims and Mons, whole
  cities torn down;

These things would never happen, were all men like
    Conscript Brown.
But fighting was my business, such thoughts were
    not for me,
I fought for rights, avenging wrongs, that all men
    might be free—
Or was it just an idle dream, this world's democracy?

In Northern Siberia, the town of Stanislau,
Humble little village, made most of mud and straw;
Where exiled politicians used to plot and scheme,
Now where hordes of bandits and cooties reign
    supreme;
Where people live in terror, and wolves howl through
    the night;
'Twas in this town of Stanislau I saw my damnedest
    fight.
Scouting for the C.E.F., along with twenty more,
Our forces were in strength to south, but we were
    sent before.
Mob armies occupied the town, upon destruction
    bent,
Our business in the section was to ascertain their
    strength.
Creeping on our bellies over frozen snow,
By the light of their campfires, I won't say all I saw,
But I saw a child half naked, midst the howling,
    drunken crowd,
I saw her lashed to make her dance, I heard her
    scream aloud;
A girl of wondrous beauty, soft form and tender years,
Her eyes were wild, beseeching, her face was lined
    with tears.
A girl abused by hundreds would make a heathen
    sore;
I saw that we were helpless—and then I saw some
    more—
A man leaped up beside me, I sprang to pull him down,

ECHOES FROM LABOR'S WARS   93

I saw his features clearly, the man was Conscript
Brown.
I saw him pass their sentries, I say him gain the
town,
I saw the mob surround him, I saw him beaten down;
Then we left the ground together, with a kind of
cursing sob,
Twenty howling demons, a shame to any mob.
My mind was kind of hazy, don't remember half the
fight,
It seemed to me a dozen times I lived and died that
night;
I was stabbed and clubbed and shot through,
sometimes up and sometimes down,
I shot and stabbed at all I saw in that cursed town.
Once, lying in a pool of blood, I fancied I was dead,
Yet when a Bolshevist went by, I shot him in the
head.
Then at last I heard a bugle. Was it fever? or I
dreamed?
Like someone blowing cook-house, far, far away it
seemed;
And I thought I rode the "bumpers" on a freight train
way back west—
'Twas the M.O. who was probing for a bullet in my
breast.
When I saw that good old khaki—say, it brought me
back to life,
I felt like one who rested after years and years of
strife.
The town was now in Christian hands, and seemed
to know it too,
Peasants smiled upon us, and I heard a rooster crow.
Our losses were not heavy, except the scouts who
fought ahead,
And I had been with them had the mob not thought
me dead.

We gathered up their bodies from different parts of
     town—
Right where the fighting started I picked up Con-
     script Brown;
Clinging to him closely was the little form, half
     dressed,
Terror frozen on her face, a dagger in her breast.
That's why I say, don't back the man who is thirsting
     for the fray,
Sometimes the heroes are the ones who have the
     least to say;
I have seen it proved a dozen times—I proved it in
     that town
Where veterans were led into hell by little Conscript
     Brown.
He is lying in Lake Ivan—'twas I who chopped his
     grave,
And I carved out with my bayonet the words, "He
     died to save."
Now when the sun—when sun there is—far off to
     west goes down,
Its last rays kind of linger on a cross marked "Con-
     script Brown."

Flags Are Pieces of Cloth

FLAGS ARE PIECES OF CLOTH. Flags are usually dyed some bright, more or less attractive colors. Some flags present certain bars and crosses, some have stars, stripes, circles, crescents, harps, dragons, orange bodies, green bodies, red bodies—and even the sinister skull and cross-bones of the notorious black flag or Jolly Roger.

In certain ways flags are useful and harmless enough. Flags on the stern of a ship are useful to tell what port that ship hails from, or on public buildings they are useful to identify the City Hall or Post Office. It is only indeed when people begin to attach a sentimental interest to flags that they become harmful and a great agency of evil. Thousands of men and women have lost their lives as a result of this sentimental interest which they allowed to become exaggerated into a kind of hysterical mania. Buckets of blood have been spilled in defense of the green flag and the orange flag, and for what those flags were supposed to represent. Rich men and capitalists with property to protect in certain foreign lands, have very cleverly arranged to drape some of these flags over such property. Often, indeed usually, the property referred to was stolen by the rich men from the natives of the country where the property is located. In an effort to recover this plunder that was stolen from them, the natives attempt to seize it forcibly, and in the process the flag that has been draped over it is pulled down.

It is then that the rich men and capitalists take advantage of the sentimental nonsense that has been taught in the public schools about the flag. They publish in the newspapers of the country—which they either own or bribe—that the flag, the piece of cloth which we love, has been outraged and insulted. This arouses us to indignant frenzy, and encouraged by the capitalists, we march or sail away to the foreign land to steal back the property that has been recovered by the natives or real owners. The wise capitalist is not the least bit interested in the piece of cloth that was pulled down, but he is interested in recovering his plunder, so he gets us to march or sail away, to suffer and die in the effort of recovering his property—all the time assuring us that what we are really doing is avenging an insult to the piece of cloth. Smooth work, eh, what?

But of course you say, "It is not the flag itself, it is what the flag represents—the beautiful principles of right and justice that the flag stands for and upholds." I answer that what the flag stands for depends entirely on who is standing under it, or who controls it. The king, the capitalist, the dictator are left to interpret what it stands for, and they make it interpret what is to their own interests. The insignia of ancient Rome stood for slavery and oppression; the flag of Spain, in its day of power, stood for plunder; the flag of the Catholic party stood for the murder and extermination of all Protestants and heretics; the orange flag of the Protestant party stood for the burning and murdering of Catholics. As one may not be permitted to speak the truth of the flag of the country in which one happens to live, I ask you just to pick up the authentic history of that country, and decide for yourself in just how many cases that flag stood for right, justice and high ideals. You will find that when the country happened to be for the time weak, it was ever whining about oppression and injustice, but in the day that it happened to be strong, it was practicing that same oppression and injustice, and calling the process "progress."

No, one may not tell the truth about some flags, but just now there is one flag that it is fashionable to discuss. Ho, there! Hold that blood-red banner high, and let us examine it. We have the advantage of being one who is supposed to be more or less familiar with it. We have had the experience of marching under that blood-red banner, and when we thus marched we had all the beautiful dreams and high ideals of the modern schoolboy, who sings in the classroom about the national flag. We interpreted what the red flag stood for to be emancipation of the working classes. To us the red flag meant liberty, justice, equality; a fair day's pay for a fair day's work. But like other flags, the red flag has different idolators to interpret it. The day came when it became clear to me that loyalty to the red flag meant that I should cut the throat of every man who did not happen to agree with me; that the hateful bourgeois must be exterminated, just as a King Henry would exterminate a Catholic, or as Queen Mary would exterminate a Protestant. Loyalty to a red flag meant that I must murder my poor old mother because she happened to have a home to shelter her in her old age.

Bah! Don't seek to blind my eyes by waving a flag in them. You ask me, would I not fight under any circumstances? I answer, Yes, I would fight for my own property; I would fight if somebody tried to take my plate of soup or my bowl of porridge; but I will not fight to recover somebody else's property, or in the interest or for the dignity of any piece of cloth. Oh, yes, I know—when you are fighting for the capitalist, you are told that what the capitalist is trying to recover is the property of the Empire, and consequently *your* property. Oh yeah, it's your property! If it is, then all I say is, TRY AND GET IT!

Part 4

"Oh, You Will Not Drive Over Ben Verick? No, Man, No!"

"Oh, You Will Not Drive Over Ben Verick? No, Man, No!"

THERE WAS A TIME more than thirty years ago (around 1923), when commercial travellers and tourists assembled around the hotels in different parts of the province of Nova Scotia would discuss their experiences, the beauty spots and what might be called the highway hazards of travel. At that date the highways left much to be desired but since then this condition has been so improved with pavement, new bridges and sign-boards as to make touring almost ideal.

But travelling, either in the old horse and buggy days or by the modern motor car, particularly in the more remote regions, is likely to recall unusual experiences. Smokey Mountain in northern Cape Breton, for instance, was a conspicuous peak on the landscape and it was not unusual for one of the group assembled in the hotels referred to, to boast that he had driven over Smokey on a dark and stormy night and landed right into Ingonish at one o'clock in the morning. The way this experience was detailed, it was quite evident that the teller had hoped for at least a murmur of applause for this daring feat.

But the fact was, and is, that while Smokey is high, one does not deserve any cheers for having scaled it, because on both sides of the highway there is very heavy vegetation and one could not drive off or fall off the mountain even if he tried to. And, as this vegetation hides the view, there is no chance of getting dizzy by looking some hundreds of feet down into the sea below. And yet for those who had never visited the area, the tale, well told, with the usual exaggeration, might leave the impression that crossing Smokey was something akin to climbing Everest or the Matterhorn.

In later years, due as stated to nearly perfect highways and excellent sport fishing prospects in northern Cape Breton plus scenic attractions, crossing Smokey is considered no more of an adventure than walking upstairs. Then came the day when the new highway thrill began to be heard of. This also was in northern Cape Breton and the craze was and still is to "go over the Cabot Trail!"

In its raw state, before it attracted the attention of the government, this Cabot Trail presented a real road hazard and several serious accidents to motorists and motor cars were reported in the press. If one kept his "eyes front" and toward the landscape, the scene was beautiful with rugged mountains, green hills and lovely valleys. But if he dared to cast his eyes down, the scene was likely to be horrible. The traveller found himself on a narrow ledge of a mountainside with the mountain towering to his left, but to his right—Ugh! a straight dip of what seemed like hundreds of feet down, down to some rocky ravine or raging sea. He just closes his eyes and prays until this particular point on the trail is passed.

The government did much to decrease the hazard by widening the trail at these danger points, but still, realizing that many travellers seek a thrill to tell their grandchildren about, they did not tame the tiger to too great an extent and nervous travellers still insist that they nearly lost their lives on the Cabot Trail.

It has been said that "familiarity breeds contempt." To drive over Smokey is no longer considered an adventure, due largely to improved highway conditions. Thousands of motor cars go over the Cabot Trail every summer season and, due again to improved road conditions, this trip is considered nothing more than an agreeable experience. But there is another hazard of the north "known to few but me." It is not along any trunk road and thus has attracted little attention, but as thirty-five years ago my duty called me into this region, I am inclined to tell you about it.

Having doubtless conquered (fear), and been over the Cabot Trail, perhaps you are seeking new worlds or mountains to conquer. Very well! Just follow me, friend.

I WAS REGISTERED at the hotel in the town of Inverness, having arrived by train, and that evening after supper I began to quiz mine host, Mr. Alex Campbell, about the territory I had to cover during the next few days. I had customers to interview all the way from this town of Inverness right down to Port Hood and most of them were in rather remote sections off the so-called beaten trail. The post road through Mabou and down to Port Hood did not interest me, as my contacts led me down the shore road through Strathlorne, Port Ban, MacKinnon's Brook and further south. It was the winter season with considerable snow, but Mr. Campbell assured me that the shore road was passable. He had talked that very day to a farmer who had driven in with horse and sleigh from Port Ban. There were, he said, no crossroads or anything to confuse a traveller. All I need do was follow the road along the shore and I should have no difficulty.

The following morning I engaged a rig at the livery stable of Johnny Owes-ther-bic—which is probably not the correct way to spell the last name, but what can one do when he is no Gaelic scholar?—and away I go down the shore road. Concluding my business at Strathlorne and at certain other scattered farm houses along the road, I drove in to the tiny village of Port Ban. It was here that I heard that dread name, "Ben Verick" {Publisher's Note: "Beinn Bhiorach," Gaelic for "Sharp Mountain"}—and I was to hear it many times before and after nightfall. Talking to a very agreeable but slightly curious resident, he asked me what my destination was after leaving his home. There is not a doubt but the gentleman meant to be helpful to the stranger at his gate and I, needing information, replied, "I am headed down to MacKinnon's Brook and beyond to Mabou."

"Oh! You are on the wrong road, you will have to

go back to Inverness and take the post road to Mabou and come into MacKinnon's Brook from the south."

"But is there not a road over the mountain?" I asked.

"You will not go over the Ben Verick?" came the shocked answer.

"I intend to," I replied.

"Oh, no! You will not go over the Ben Verick. No, no!"

"But they told me at the hotel and the livery stable man said there was a road over."

"Oh, no, man. The ice from the top of the mountain runs over that narrow road and to the right it is a clear drop of hundreds of feet straight down and into the sea. Oh, no. You will not go over the Ben Verick."

I did not argue further with the gentleman but thanked him for his kindness. I had other customers further down the road and I determined to call on these and then if necessary turn back and approach MacKinnon's Brook from the south as I had been advised.

Naturally, at the other houses I pursued my inquiries and at many met the dread warning, "You will not go over the Ben Verick! No, man, no." But it seemed as I came nearer to the dread mountain, the natives seemed to be losing respect for it—perhaps proving again that "familiarity breeds contempt." I also learned the reason or excuse for this secondary road. Most of the settlers along this northern shore had business contacts in Inverness town and this road or trail was to accommodate them. As the shore became settled further south the road was extended until it came right down to the Ben Verick. Those living on the south side of the mountain did not relish the idea of going back to Mabou to catch the trunk road to Inverness, either. They could not tunnel through the mountain, so they cut a ledge along the side of it facing the sea. In the summertime when there was no ice, a person with a good steady head and a good steady horse could pass along this ledge, there being just room for the width of a carriage and with perhaps a few inches to spare.

AS ONE APPROACHED THE MOUNTAIN from either side it was evident that the residents did not like to have it referred to as impassable. There was a legend that many years before two young men belonging to the section but who had been out west came home to visit their friends. They and two bottles of Scotch whiskey drove over the Ben Verick in the pitch dark in an old Ford car. And did not Sandy Beaton from the Brook bring a thrashing machine over the Ben Verick? And did not his daughter "Marack" drive a load of hay over it? No, these good people felt that any dangerous feature lessened the value of their property—something like a haunted house will be avoided. They did not wish to have their happy community shunned.

At a home I visited as I approached nearer to the mountain I discussed the possibility of the crossing and getting down into the valley below. The farmer at this home seemed to have even less respect for the Ben Verick than those who lived further back along the trail. This gentleman declared that if there was no ice at this particular point and if I had a good steady head and a good steady horse I might make the crossing. But he advised that I stop at the McDonald home which was the last farm on this side of the mountain and enquire of these good people as to the condition at the narrow point of the trail. "One of the McDonald boys will inform you of this and he will probably attempt the crossing with you, if conditions seem favourable." And it is one of the McDonald boys who is the real hero of this tale. As I drove toward this home I noticed that the road led upward and it was evident that I was climbing a sharp hill or mountain and doubtless nearing the dreaded Ben Verick.

Looking at my watch I found that it was about nine P.M. and a very dark night. At the McDonald house my knock attracted a young man to the door and I was invited inside. I explained my problem and at once young McDonald volunteered to go with me and investigate the condition on the mountain.

"There has been a recent thaw," he explained, "and if the road is icy at the danger point your sleigh might slip down and carry you and the horse with it into the depths below. Is your horse sharp?" the young man enquired. He then lighted an oil lantern and I noticed that he hastily grabbed a hatchet or a small hand-axe, then he said, "Come on. Let's go!"

As we drove higher and higher up the incline I began to get nervous and I suggested to my new friend that perhaps he had better take the reins and guide the horse, as he would be aware of the danger points.

"Oh, there is no danger here," the young man assured me. "It is only at one point near the top of the mountain. If you could see here, you would find that there is trees and vegetation on each side of us and we could not leave the road if we tried, but near the top, where the old folks cut the ledge years ago, the road is bare slatey shale. I guess the water from the mountain top came down the side all through the years and washed all the good earth away, and nothing grows in this rock formation. That is why one needs a sharp, well-shod horse in crossing the Ben Verick in the wintertime. Drive on, Mister, I will tell you when we come to the bad place and then maybe we will have to lead the horse. It will be in our favor if the animal is steady and does not stop or balk at the bad part of the road. It is perhaps better for him and better for us that it is so dark and we cannot see the right side of the road where it dips down straight into the sea. Of course, I have driven over this mountain in the daytime before and, if you can trust your animal, there is really no danger."

After we had proceeded a bit further, with me still driving, my friend said, "Now, you stop the horse and wait here. The place is just beyond. I will go ahead and see about the condition of the road." After taking the axe with him, McDonald proceeded up the trail. Returning after some minutes he instructed me, "Leave the horse and sleigh here and you come with me."

"Is the road icy?" I asked with apprehension.

"Some ice, but we will see," he answered bravely.

Proceeding further, at one point he got down on his hands and knees and I could hear him chopping with the axe. Then he said, "We better leave the sleigh on the mountain for the night. I am afraid it will slip. But you unhitch the animal and wait here." I did as instructed and he soon returned with further instructions. "Now I will lead the horse by the head and you follow me."

Soon we halted again, and again McDonald descended to his knees, remarking, "Now, Mister, right here is the bad place. I am going to crawl across. You take the reins out through the rings at the animal's middle and leave them attached only at the bridle so they will be long. Catch the end of the reins in your hand and crawl after me, keeping very close to your left and in close to the rib of the mountain. I will meet you and take the end of the reins from you. I am afraid to walk with the animal in case he shies or balks and we both go over the side."

I handed him the reins when we met near the middle of the "bad place" and he instructed me to crawl back to safety. He also crawled to safety on the other side with the ends of the reins in his hand. Then I heard him say, "Gid up. Come on boy." The gallant steed obeyed and soon I had a triumphant call from my guide. "All right, Mister. Now you can crawl over here and don't be afraid—the ice is well chopped and the distance is not great. You can now lead the horse down to Sandy's. It is only a short distance to the valley below and there are no bad places."

AND IT WAS THUS THAT I CROSSED the Ben Verick. One thing I always regretted was that I do not ever recall thanking my good friend or rewarding him in any way for his kindness and care. I was excited, nervous and shaky after the experience, but I thank God that it was at night I made the crossing. When I viewed the "bad spot" the next morning I had another attack of nerves. Ugh! It still makes me nervous to think about it. But I admit this weakness. I have no head for high places and cannot cross an ordinary railway trestle without my stomach turning inside out. And so the heroes of the crossing were young McDonald and the sensible livery stable horse of Johnny Owes-ther-bic.

In those days I had much experience with livery stable horses and still have kindly memories of many that I have driven. They had courage, honesty and intelligence to a remarkable degree. I remember driving one dark, stormy night down in Lunenburg County with a big grey livery stable horse. It was wet snow that blinded me, and one would think blinded the horse. There was a large leather apron with the rig and in this were two slits to place the reins through. I was twelve miles from my destination when the storm struck and the snow was just blinding. I placed the reins through the holes, held on with my head and hands under the robe, and let the horse go as he pleased. There were various turns and crossroads on this highway but I rode on for a couple of hours, trusting to the animal that kept going at a good smart pace. Here and there from the motion of the wagon I could tell that he was making a turn or going over a bridge or railway crossing. After a time he halted and I was astonished to discover that he had carried me right to the door of his own stable. It must have been instinct that guided him home, for nothing living could see through that thick snow.

On another occasion, in a neighboring province, I used to drive a little mare named "Lady," and she was just that, a perfect lady. I was always glad to see her and chose her when I was driving in that section—and she seemed pleased to see me. I used to feed her sugar at the country grocery stores and I got the impression that she used to stop at these stores, expecting a treat. On another dark but stormy night I was driving in a section where the road was level and in good condition. Suddenly Lady halted and refused to go further, even when I touched her with the whip. This was very puzzling and, alighting from the rig, I went to her head and began to lead her by the bridle. Fifty feet from where she halted I learned the cause. There was a big tree across the road and Lady, not being a steeplechaser, did not attempt to jump. Certainly she could not see it. It was at a curve of the road and the night was very dark. Animal instinct, again, I presume. But as is the weakness of many old men, I am straying from the telling of my tale.

MY SLEIGH, OF COURSE, had been left up on the mountain on the other side of the "bad place," so when parting from McDonald I led the horse by the bridle down the mountain and into the valley below. My destination was the home of Mr. Sandy Beaton. I had met Mr. Beaton on another occasion at the hotel in Mabou. We had shared a wee drop of Scotch and I had been urged to visit at his home at the first or any opportunity, and as I expected, I was warmly received.

"Where did you come from, Fraser, man?" Mr. Beaton wanted to know. He was puzzled to see me, leading a harnessed horse with no vehicle behind him and in the dead of night.

"Down over the mountain," I replied. Now that the danger seemed past I was inclined to be a little proud of my experience.

"And is that the way you travel now—leading an animal with no sleigh or wagon?"

"I left the sleigh up on the mountain." And then I proceeded to give some detail of my adventure.

Coming to the defense of his mountain and the locality in general, Mr. Beaton pooh-poohed the idea that there was any danger in crossing the Ben Verick. "I go over it to Inverness town most every weekend," he added. Sandy took care of my faithful horse and the ladies prepared a good supper, after which there was a general demand that I "tell all the news."

I have always found people in the rural districts very hospitable and easy to entertain. Any story or joke that would seem like a "thrice-told tale" in the town or city, would go over big among these good people—the reason probably being that, busy with the endless work of a farm, they had little time to read the papers or listen to the radio. But mine host, loyal to his homeland, seemed at odds with the powers that be. He felt that highways were neglected, that his mountain road could be widened and made more attractive at very little expense, and this would be a great convenience for the people who were much attracted to the largest town of Inverness County.

"Perhaps you don't vote right, Sandy," I suggested—and his answer to this was prompt and a little bitter.

"That is just the trouble, Fraser. We Beatons, Rankins, McDonalds and other Scottish families in these parts always supported the present government. But the government concludes that the Beatons and Rankins and McDonalds are all good, faithful friends who would scorn to 'turn their coats,' so we will seek new converts to support us and thus swell our majority. Acting on this, they fix roads elsewhere and neglect their good friends here."

Another observation of mine in the rural (areas is) that the people there seemed more intelligent than in the towns and cities. Perhaps they are not so poisoned with propaganda by the press, advertising mediums, etc. They don't believe, for instance, that every different kind of tobacco can be superior to every other, or that Soapso is better than Sudso, or vice versa. If one believes all he hears or reads, it weakens the intellect. If I declare to a ruralite that forty dollars per month is not sufficient to maintain a family of four, the gentleman will always agree with me. But if I make the same statement in the city or town, I am called a "RED."

Another thing I soon discovered was that the Beaton home did not lack for entertainment. The young lady of the family, Miss Mary Beaton, was a talented performer on the violin, and during the course of the evening Sandy urged her to get her fiddle and play for Fraser, whom he doubted was a true Scot. And the young lady, laying the violin across her knee, charmed us with "Lord MacDonald," " The Lament of Wullie Wallace," and many other pleasing airs that I could not identify.

Then Sandy looked at me suspiciously, winked at his charming daughter and urged, "Marack, Oughs-than Frishell, Oughs-Frishell."

Smiling with mischief, Miss Beaton let loose with another air that I did not recognize. I learned afterwards that with the first notes of "Oughs-than Fri-shell" it was expected that I would leap to my feet and do a Highland Fling. But I disappointed my friend Sandy and was promptly aware of his disappointment.

"Don't you know that tune, man? You are no Scotsman and no Fraser!" And Sandy scorned to relieve me of my ignorance. However, I learned later that Oughs-than Frishell was the favorite pibroch of the Fraser clan, and that Sandy was justified in considering me something of a half-breed when I did not recognize it.

After a pleasant evening spent with music and story, I was led to the guest chamber by mine host, who hoped I would say my prayers, rest well, and assured me that in the morning we would recover my sleigh from the top of the mountain.

And of course the morning came, as mornings will and, gazing around me from the little valley, I was astonished to observe the mountains in this particular section of Cape Breton Island.

Many years before, while reading geography at school, I learned that the Cobequid Mountains on the Nova Scotia mainland were referred to as the chief heights in the province. But I do not recall any mention of the Inverness mountains in this Cape Mabou section of the county. Since that time I have observed the Cobequid Mountains and passed through the Canadian Rockies. These latter are of course higher, but the former seemed to me just ordinary green hills.

I have heard mountains referred to as "rugged," but think those of this section of Inverness would be better called "ragged." They seemed to lack regularity—seemed like one mountain piled on top of another in disorder—one tottering on its toes and another balancing on its ear as if dissatisfied to remain in its present position. Passing below these, one was inclined to duck his head in the fear that a large section of the universe was about to tumble down on top of him. From such a scene a timid man is glad to escape, and after Sandy reharnessed the horse we started up the mountain to recover my sleigh. I noticed that while Sandy led the horse with one hand grasping the bridle, in the other hand he carried a long, stout rope, and because he kept assuring me that we would have no difficulty, I felt that he might himself have some doubts in the matter.

Climbing the rough road that I had descended the night before in the dark, we finally came to what I recognized as "the bad place." I could see marks in the icy surface where McDonald had hacked into it the night before. On my right hand was the bare, slaty mountain, in front of me the narrow ledge, and at my left a straight drop, I know not how many feet or yards, down, down into the sea below. It made me sick to look. Guess I grew pale at the prospect of crossing that devil's dip.

Noticing my hesitation, Sandy asked, "Are you scared, man?" And then added, "I admit, some don't like it. But we must get across. You catch my coat-tail, keep close to the rib—don't look down or stop. Better close your eyes and think of something else."

It was, after all, not a long trip, and after taking perhaps fifty steps behind Sandy, I heard him say, "There, now, that was not so bad." Then I opened my eyes, but my legs were shaky and my stomach rushing up into my throat. Observing me, Sandy said, "Take a rest, man. Wish I had a drop of brandy." Sandy then went back to observe the ice on the trail. Some moisture from the upper mountain had made the ice slippery. There were no ruts like on well-travelled roads to hold the sleigh runners in a kind of groove, and I could see my friend feared that the sleigh would slip down into the depths below. It was then I realized why Sandy had carried the rope. He now went and attached one end of it to the outside runner of the sleigh, hitched the horse to the vehicle and gave me my further instructions.

"Now, Fraser, I will get in the sleigh and drive over slowly, and you hold this rope and feed it out, also slowly, so as not to let the sleigh runner slip over the side. You are quite safe here and so am I in the sleigh. Only for the damn ice there would be nothing to it."

Of course, due to Sandy's plan and the sense of the horse, the crossing was accomplished. Sandy was delighted with himself and hopped back over the trail to my side like a toe-dancer. The only problem left was to get me back to the other side and strangely enough now the prospect of crossing did not seem so terrifying. On these pages I have somewhat enslaved the expression, "familiarity breeds contempt," and here again it was to some extent proven. It is always the prospect of danger that chills and not the experience. Many people fear the dentist, but are astonished to find, after they get into his chair, that he is not such a bad fellow. It is not on record that men experience much fear in battle, but the thought of receiving a bullet or bayonet thrust is very disagreeable. I recall a story I read of a naval man who was on a torpedoed ship. He described vividly how the ship turned over as he slid down the side; but what he though peculiar was that he did not experience fear, but rather was disappointed to see his nice new service-cap leave his head and slide into the ocean before him.

Still (or again) clinging to Sandy's coat-tail, I re-crossed the "bad place" and we drove down the trail to the house. But would I drive over the Ben Verick again? No, man, no!

Conclusion

My days and nights of labor done,
Come over, friends, and meet my son;
This product of my fancy wild,
You'll find him, perhaps, a forward child—
With caustic quips and vulgar rhymes—
He was conceived in sinful times
And poisoned by life's foul air—
It's shocking, ma'am, to hear him swear
And rave in manner unrefined—
His father had an outlawed mind.
He was not born like any other,
The poor boy never had a mother.
Would you expect the normal where
There lacks a mother's loving care?
Could he be gentle like the rest,
Flung from a father's bitter breast?

And yet there's points about the child
That might excuse his seeming wild,
His lack of tact, restraint, devotion—
He is a product of emotion
And life to him is not what it seems—
His days are spent in wildest dreams,
And on his pillow, half the night
He worries over wrong and right.
A fisher fills his net some morn—
The prize from him is quickly torn.
A murderer hangs—a poor man he—
A wealthy murderer goes free.
The miners dug yon bank of coal,
But that same day 'twas from them stole.
A child outside wedlock is born—
Alone the mother bears the scorn.

Observing this, my child must then
Much marvel at the ways of men,

And from his pages, leaf by leaf,
He will labor to expose the thief;
Poor innocent will strive to show
To men what they already know,
And what they choose to tolerate—
Abuse of power by the great,
The slaughtered right, the nourished wrong,
The tortured weak, the pampered strong—
Poor foolish child, to worry so
About the world and all its woe;
Lay down your pen, I charge you, boy,
It is a silly useless toy;
That pen's too blunt, that ink too thin
To heal a world so steeped in sin.

And is the effort worth the time
One spends in protest and in rhyme?
As gaily pass the careless crowd
Some are heard to laugh aloud
As those who hate to hear the truth—
And all ignore the wailing youth.
For of his lineage 'tis said
His father was a horrid Red;
My literary race is run—
I swear I'll breed no other son.
Dance on, old mad and dizzy earth,
I'll strangle my next book at birth—
"A worthy deed—small loss," says you,
"You should have strangled this one too!"

I Will Drive No Bargains With My God

I will drive no bargains with my God,
The sun don't barter with the sod,
The plants and flowers, every one,
Make no demands upon the sun,
But rather like this soul of mine
Are grateful when it deigns to shine.

I have heard some Christian preachers say
That they were saved and only they,
I have heard some Christian choir airs
Sing they were God's and God was theirs,
Such bold presumption seemed to me
Not due respect but vanity.

I will drive no bargains with my God,
I'll soon be blended with the sod,
And patient in the sod I'll wait
To learn, my soul, your final fate.
Should outraged deity claim its due,
My soul, my soul—ah, woe to you.